Acceptance and Commitment Therapy

Theories of Psychotherapy Series

Theories of Psychotherapy Series

Jon Carlson and Matt Englar-Carlson, Series Editors

Acceptance and Commitment Therapy

Steven C. Hayes and Jason Lillis

American Psychological Association

Washington, DC

Published by
American Psychological Association
750 First Street, NE
Washington, DC 20002
www.apa.org

To order
APA Order Department
P.O. Box 92984
Washington, DC 20090-2984
Tel: (800) 374-2721; Direct: (202) 336-5510
Fax: (202) 336-5502; TDD/TTY: (202) 336-6123
Online: www.apa.org/pubs/books
E-mail: order@apa.org

In the U.K., Europe, Africa, and the Middle East, copies may be ordered from
American Psychological Association
3 Henrietta Street
Covent Garden, London
WC2E 8LU England

Typeset in Minion by Circle Graphics, Columbia, MD

Printer: Edwards Brothers, Inc., Ann Arbor, MI
Cover Designer: Minker Design, Sarasota, FL
Cover Art: *Lily Rising,* 2005, oil and mixed media on panel in craquelure frame, by Betsy Bauer

The opinions and statements published are the responsibility of the authors, and such opinions and statements do not necessarily represent the policies of the American Psychological Association.

Library of Congress Cataloging-in-Publication Data

Hayes, Steven C.
  Acceptance and commitment therapy / Steven C. Hayes and Jason Lillis. — 1st ed.
    p. cm. — (Theories of psychotherapy)
  Includes bibliographical references and index.
  ISBN 978-1-4338-1153-1 — ISBN 1-4338-1153-7-1. Acceptance and commitment therapy. I. Lillis, Jason. II. Title.
  RC489.A32H39 2012
  616.891425—dc23
                                2012001150

British Library Cataloguing-in-Publication Data
A CIP record is available from the British Library.

Printed in the United States of America
First Edition

For my son, Little Stevie: I hope that when life gets difficult you
will find a way to be accepting of who you really are.

—*Steven C. Hayes*

For my wife, Katie, for being my loving companion on the journey
and for always making sure we don't lose our way.

—*Jason Lillis*

Contents

Series Preface

Some might argue that in the contemporary clinical practice of psychotherapy, evidence-based intervention and effective outcome have overshadowed theory in importance. Maybe. But, as the editors of this series, we don't propose to take up that controversy here. We do know that psychotherapists adopt and practice according to one theory or another because their experience, and decades of good evidence, suggests that having a sound theory of psychotherapy leads to greater therapeutic success. Still, the role of theory in the helping process can be hard to explain. This narrative about solving problems helps convey theory's importance:

> Aesop tells the fable of the sun and wind having a contest to decide who was the most powerful. From above the earth, they spotted a man walking down the street, and the wind said that he bet he could get his coat off. The sun agreed to the contest. The wind blew, and the man held on tightly to his coat. The more the wind blew, the tighter he held. The sun said it was his turn. He put all of his energy into creating warm sunshine, and soon the man took off his coat.

What does a competition between the sun and the wind to remove a man's coat have to do with theories of psychotherapy? We think this deceptively simple story highlights the importance of theory as the precursor to any effective intervention—and hence to a favorable outcome. Without a guiding theory we might treat the symptom without understanding the role of the individual. Or we might create power conflicts with our clients and not understand that, at times, indirect means of helping (sunshine) are often as effective—if not more so—than direct ones (wind). In the absence of theory, we might lose track of the treatment rationale and instead get caught up in, for example, social correctness and not wanting to do something that looks too simple.

What exactly *is* theory? The *APA Dictionary of Psychology* defines theory as "a principle or body of interrelated principles that purports to explain or predict a number of interrelated phenomena." In psychotherapy, a theory is a set of principles used to explain human thought and behavior, including what causes people to change. In practice, a theory creates the goals of therapy and specifies how to pursue them. Haley (1997) noted that a theory of psychotherapy ought to be simple enough for the average therapist to understand, but comprehensive enough to account for a wide range of eventualities. Furthermore, a theory guides action toward successful outcomes while generating hope in both the therapist and client that recovery is possible.

Theory is the compass that allows psychotherapists to navigate the vast territory of clinical practice. In the same ways that navigational tools have been modified to adapt to advances in thinking and ever-expanding territories to explore, theories of psychotherapy have changed over time. The different schools of theories are commonly referred to as waves, the first wave being psychodynamic theories (i.e., Adlerian, psychoanalytic), the second wave learning theories (i.e., behavioral, cognitive–behavioral), the third wave humanistic theories (person-centered, gestalt, existential), the fourth wave feminist and multicultural theories, and the fifth wave postmodern and constructivist theories. In many ways, these waves represent how psychotherapy has adapted and responded to changes in psychology, society, and epistemology as well as to changes in the nature of psychotherapy itself. Psychotherapy and the theories that guide it are dynamic and responsive. The wide variety of theories is also testament to the different ways in which the same human behavior can be conceptualized (Frew & Spiegler, 2008).

It is with these two concepts in mind—the central importance of theory and the natural evolution of theoretical thinking—that we developed the APA Theories of Psychotherapy Series. Both of us are thoroughly fascinated by theory and the range of complex ideas that drive each model. As university faculty members who teach courses on the theories of psychotherapy, we wanted to create learning materials that not only highlight the essence of the major theories for professionals and professionals in training but also clearly bring the reader up to date on the current status of the models. Often in books on theory, the biography of the original theorist overshadows the evolution of the model. In contrast, our intent is to highlight the contemporary uses of the theories as well as their history and context.

As this project began, we faced two immediate decisions: which theories to address and who best to present them. We looked at graduate-level theories of psychotherapy courses to see which theories are being taught, and we explored popular scholarly books, articles, and conferences to determine which theories draw the most interest. We then developed a dream list of authors from among the best minds in contemporary theoretical practice. Each author is one of the leading proponents of that approach as well as a knowledgeable practitioner. We asked each author to review the core constructs of the theory, bring the theory into the modern sphere of clinical practice by looking at it through a context of evidence-based practice, and clearly illustrate how the theory looks in action.

There are 24 titles planned for the series. Each title can stand alone or can be put together with a few other titles to create materials for a course in psychotherapy theories. This option allows instructors to create a course featuring the approaches they believe are the most salient today. To support this end, APA Books has also developed a DVD for each of the approaches that demonstrates the theory in practice with a real client. Many of the DVDs show therapy over six sessions. Contact APA Books for a complete list of available DVD programs (http://www.apa.org/pubs/videos).

Acceptance and commitment therapy (ACT) is rapidly becoming one of the most popular therapies in the world. As you read this important book you will soon understand why. It is a practical, cognitive-behavioral approach that stresses Eastern concepts of mindfulness and acceptance with Western behavioral change and commitment strategies. The goal of ACT is to produce psychological flexibility. This therapy process leads the client to learn to flow with life and learn to just notice thoughts, feelings and actions and then create the needed behavioral steps to bring them in line with their core values. In this volume, one of the founders of ACT, Steven C. Hayes works with Jason Lillis to provide a primer that will help you to understand the approach and why it is gaining such strong professional support. This volume is an important addition to the series.

—Jon Carlson and Matt Englar-Carlson

REFERENCES

Frew, J., & Spiegler, M. (2008). *Contemporary psychotherapies for a diverse world.* Boston, MA: Lahaska Press.

Haley, J. (1997). *Leaving home: The therapy of disturbed young people.* New York, NY: Routledge.

How to Use This Book With APA Psychotherapy Videos

Each book in the Theories of Psychotherapy Series is specifically paired with a DVD that demonstrates the theory applied in actual therapy with a real client. Many DVDs feature the author of the book as the guest therapist, allowing students to see eminent scholars and practitioners putting the theory they write about into action.

The DVDs have a number of features that make them useful for learning more about theoretical concepts:

- Many DVDs contain six full sessions of psychotherapy over time, giving viewers a chance to see how clients respond to the application of the theory over the course of several sessions.
- Each DVD has a brief introductory discussion recapping the basic features of the theory behind the approach demonstrated. This allows viewers to review the key aspects of the approach about which they have just read.
- DVDs feature actual clients in unedited psychotherapy sessions. This provides an opportunity to get a sense of the look and feel of real psychotherapy, something that written case examples and transcripts sometimes cannot convey.
- There is a therapist commentary track that viewers may choose to play during the psychotherapy sessions. This track gives insight into why therapists do what they do in a session. Further, it provides an in vivo opportunity to see how the therapist uses the model to conceptualize the client.

The books and DVDs together make a powerful teaching tool for showing how theoretical principles affect practice. In the case of this book, the DVD *Acceptance and Commitment Therapy*, which features the lead author of this book as the guest expert, provides a vivid example of what this approach looks and sounds like in practice. In this single session DVD, Dr. Hayes works with an African American woman coping with multiple health concerns and struggling with not living up to the expectations of her mother. Dr. Hayes works with her to accept her emotions, to use mindfulness to observe her thoughts, and to live a life in which her actions are guided by her own values rather than feelings of guilt.

Preface

Since its inception nearly 30 years ago, acceptance and commitment therapy (ACT) and its underlying theory of human cognition have gradually assumed a role of importance in cognitive behavior therapy, in behavior analysis, and in the empirically supported treatments more generally. In this book, we try to explain what ACT is and where it came from. We discuss the philosophy and theory behind it. We describe the model of psychopathology, human flourishing, and intervention. We show some of its methods, and we characterize the data related to it. We make use of therapy transcripts throughout; some of these are composites, but many are actual session transcripts, edited for clarity and confidentiality.

ACT was first roughly formulated around 1980 by Steven Hayes. ACT was developed into a more organized system by Steven's students and colleagues, including especially Kirk Strosahl and Kelly Wilson (coauthors of the original book on ACT in 1999). Jason Lillis, coauthor of this volume, is a former student.

We have structured this book as a conversation. We refer to the reader as *you* and the authors—at times including our colleagues in the field—as *we*. We the authors briefly peek into the future and challenge you, the reader, to consider being part of it. We hope to open up this approach enough to enable you to know whether or not it resonates with you. If we are successful, at the end of this short volume you will know whether it might be worth your time to spend more energy on understanding ACT.

The book includes a useful list of technical terms in the Glossary, some of which will not be needed to engage with our discussion of ACT here but may prove helpful with other works in the field.

Our goal is to have a conversation that will help you understand ACT and perhaps consider how it might better contribute to the well-being and progress of clients. We hope to expose you not just to the intellectual basis of the work (the head), and not just to the technical methods, both borrowed and new, within the ACT work (the hands), but also to the heart of the work.

ACT is about the deepest issues that all people face. Welcome. Have a seat. Let's talk about psychology. Let's talk about life. Let's talk about why it is hard to be human and what we might do to make it easier.

Acceptance and Commitment Therapy

1

Introduction

Why is it so hard to be human? This question is central to the field of psychotherapy and to psychology as a whole. Compared with other living creatures, we are spectacularly successful in a material sense, and yet even amidst plenty, there are spectacularly high rates of psychological misery. It is difficult for people to flourish as whole human beings.

Humans are used to thinking of themselves as special. A magazine cover asks, "Are there other forms of intelligent life in the universe?" Few will stop to notice the self-evaluation that this question represents. It could just as well have asked, "Are there others in the universe so grand as we?"

We should not be too critical of the instinct. We *are* unusual. We are the species that imagines things that have never been. We paint beautiful paintings, create elaborate mathematical systems, reach for the stars. In the world outside the skin we are masters at solving problems.

And yet we struggle. Our mastery of the world only makes the question of human suffering more urgent, more amazing, and more poignant: *Why is it so hard to be human?* Even human beings with every imaginable advantage in the external world still can feel empty, alone, afraid, or miserable. They can turn their lives over to addiction, or compulsion, or delusion. They can struggle in their relationships and be tempted by thoughts of suicide. The ubiquity of human suffering is shocking, even in the most developed countries. Nothing in the external world is enough to guarantee health, growth, and happiness. What is hard about being human is not on the outside—it is on the inside.

In psychotherapy, we have become used to the idea of thinking of psychiatric syndromes as the source of human suffering. They are a pitifully inadequate answer to the question of suffering. They are an "answer" at all only because we don't stop to think about what syndromes are.

Syndromes are just collections of signs (things you can see) and symptoms (things people complain about). We can see drug use, for example, or listen as people complain about feelings of sadness. Signs and symptoms are, in other words, features of human misery. We are interested in syndromes because we hope that it may prove useful to organize these features into chunks under labels. But as soon as those chunks are given a name, and we begin to say that people have them, or we claim that we can prevent or cure them, they become things that can make other things happen—maybe even the very signs and symptoms that they do nothing but name.

That sequence is an illusion of language called *reification*. By definition, syndromes do not and cannot explain suffering and disability because at best they are merely forms of suffering and disability. Phenomena do not explain themselves. It would be like saying, "The reason why it is hard to be human is that it is hard *like this,* and it is hard *like that.*" This is not a legitimate answer to a "why" question.

The study of syndromes does have a larger purpose: It is designed to lead ultimately to answers about the "why" question. By systematically and carefully grouping signs and symptoms we hope to learn where these features come from (their etiology), how they develop over time (their course), and what to do about them (response to treatment). When that happens, syndromes have become *diseases:* collections of signs and symptoms with a known etiology, course, and responses to treatment, known by a single label.

Diseases are legitimate explanations of pathology, and if psychiatric syndromes led to the discovery of diseases reliably, there would be nothing to complain about. An undeniable instance of a psychiatric syndrome becoming a disease was a psychotic disorder called *general paresis.* Its signs included abnormality in eye pupil reflexes, muscular reflex abnormalities, seizures, memory impairment, and psychotic behavior. It was suspected in the 1850s that it was attributable to syphilis, and, finally, 100 years ago syphilitic spirochetes were found in the brains of those suffering from this disease. A Nobel Prize for Medicine was won for learning that inducing malaria could sometimes cure it. The invention of antibiotics later provided a more humane solution.

That is how the model is supposed to work, but it is an exception that proves a sad rule. There are only a few arguable examples of psychiatric syndromes leading to the discovery of specific psychiatric diseases as a cause, and none of the labels that roll so easily off the tongue of a psychology undergraduate fresh from a class on abnormal psychology—depression, schizophrenia, alcoholism, obsessive–compulsive disorder, and so on—are diseases, nor are they likely ever to be such. The initial rush of enthusiasm for the possibilities of the human genome project has driven more nails into this coffin: We now know that the genetic influences on these syndromes come from so many genes (they are massively "polygenetic") that they outstrip our methods for analyzing genetic influences in humans. In some cases we also now know that changes in gene expression produced by psychological and environmental influences, some of which are heritable but not through DNA (what are termed *epigenetic influences*), can be far more important than the mere presence or absence of genes, but epigenesis itself is barely understood. Given the known complexity of genetic, epigenetic, psychological, and cultural factors, the possibility of major psychiatric syndromes such as schizophrenia or depression acquiring the status of diseases in the foreseeable future approaches zero. Having a strategy work once every century or so can hardly be called real progress. It is simply not true that we know that it is hard to be human *because* of syndromes.

Well, then, why is it? We need answers or at least an approach that can lead to them.

In the area of physical medicine, studying syndromes does not always lead to an answer to the "why." The syndromal strategy tends to fail when an etiological process or small related set of such processes gives rise to many, many different outcomes, or when a single outcome comes from many different processes. In those cases, progress has usually emerged more from the lab than the clinic, as basic research is used to identify how processes work. For example, a very wide variety of environmental insults can alter the genes that regulate cell growth and lead to cancer of many different forms. This insight did not come from botanizing many different forms of cancer; it came from a basic laboratory understanding of the processes involved in cell growth.

One psychotherapy that has taken an inductive, process-oriented approach to understanding human misery and failures to prosper is Acceptance and Commitment Therapy, or ACT (Hayes, Strosahl, & Wilson, 1999, 2011; *ACT* has always been pronounced as a word, not initials, perhaps because it otherwise sounds like the abbreviation for electroconvulsive therapy, ECT.) An ACT approach is centrally focused on the grand question we began with, but it has pursued a different possible answer: that a small set of normal and necessary psychological processes can give rise to human suffering or limits to human flourishing. These ideas have been pursued in the lab, not just in the clinic. ACT researchers believe they have discovered part of why we suffer despite our special abilities: These special abilities themselves have properties that can easily lead to psychopathology and human limitation. We will begin to explain what these abilities are in the next chapter, and so begin to answer our grand question in a way other than the mainstream syndromal strategy.

Even before we get into these specifics, however, it is fun to note how this idea turns the grand question upside down. From an ACT conception, that magazine cover we started with might also have usefully read, "Are there other neurotic and unnecessarily rigid life forms in the universe?"

WHAT IS ACT?

ACT is a contextual behavioral approach to intervention that uses acceptance and mindfulness processes and commitment and behavior change processes to produce psychological flexibility. *Psychological flexibility* is the ability to experience thoughts, feelings, sensations, and memories without needless defense; as they are, not as what they say they are; and (based on what the situation affords) to persist or change in behavior in the service of chosen values.

Psychological flexibility is said to be composed of six related processes: acceptance, cognitive defusion, flexible attention to the present moment, a perspective-taking sense of self, chosen values, and committed action. The psychological flexibility model is based on behavioral principles and a behavioral theory of language and cognition known as *relational frame theory* (RFT; Hayes, Barnes-Holmes, & Roche, 2001). ACT and RFT are part of a larger development strategy called a *contextual behavioral science* (CBS) approach (Hayes, Levin, Plumb, Boulanger, & Pistorello, in press; Vilardaga, Hayes, Levin, & Muto, 2009), which is based on functional contextual thinking as is found in behavior analysis but expanded in several ways (Biglan & Hayes, 1996). The goal of CBS is the development of a comprehensive and coherent approach to psychology that is more adequate to the challenge of the human condition.

Psychology as a field is filled with polarities and overlapping questions. Is it the study of mind or of behavior? Is it a basic science or an applied science? Is clinical psychology an art, or is it a science? Scores of such questions surround the field. In the context of such questions, ACT is hard at times to categorize. It emerges from an island in the academic archipelago—contextual behavioral psychology—that is rarely visited by the mainstream and even more rarely understood. As a result, ACT can look odd from the outside.

Despite its strong behavioral roots, ACT is arguably the only major clinical approach that has spun off a comprehensive basic experimental program in cognition, RFT. Despite its affinity for basic science, ACT is a deeply experiential approach that looks from the outside more like gestalt therapy, existential therapy, humanistic, or even analytic approaches than behavior therapy. Despite the fact that ACT is part of the evidence-based therapy movement, ACT researchers are deeply critical of the idea that progress in clinical science can be based primarily on randomized controlled trials linked to manualized treatment for syndromes. People initially encountering ACT are often fascinated by its clinical techniques, and yet those who are developing ACT often do not seem that interested in techniques per se. They are more interested in its development strategy—CBS—and its set of putative processes of change—psychological flexibility.

All of this ensures that ACT is a square peg that may initially be hard to push into your existing intellectual round holes. Your experience in trying to understand ACT will parallel in some ways the initial impact of ACT on clients. It is likely to be a bit disorienting.

ACT attempts to target the dominant, problem-solving mode of mind that literal language and cognition seem to lead toward so easily. From an ACT perspective, this mode of mind is not the only or the best way to address many human problems. That very fact is paradoxical: People come to therapy because of their problems. Going to therapy is itself a problem-solving strategy. And yet ACT is skeptical about the universal applicability of problem solving.

If you wanted to put ACT into a nutshell, imagine a woman who is deeply immersed in her problems. She is sitting with a clipboard in front of her face, busily writing down the features of her problem and hoping a solution will emerge that will guide her actions. The clipboard is held tight and close—as if the answer to her problems might leap out of a close inspection of the current set of written features. She is nervously and busily parsing her thoughts about the right problem-solving approach and is waiting to change her life until the right solutions are found.

Instead of adding yet more material to the clipboard, ACT attempts to move the clipboard away from the face. Instead of providing new analyses of how the features of suffering written there suggest new problem-solving strategies, ACT attempts to help the person see the cost of focusing on the clipboard. Instead of waiting for a solution, ACT focuses on living a life passionately connected to that individual's values, *now*.

A CASE EXAMPLE

George was a 28-year-old single Hispanic mechanical engineer who had been struggling with panic disorder for 10 years. He lived in a small house owned by his alcoholic father, with whom he had a conflict-filled relationship. He blamed his father's lifelong criticism and demand for control for his deep sense of insecurity. Unable to hold a regular job because of his anxiety, he lived modestly on royalties from two successful mechanical patents. He filed additional patents periodically, always hoping for what he called "a big strike" that would make him rich and admired.

George had developed strategies to deal with his anxiety. He had traveled no more than 10 or 15 miles from home for 5 years. Although highly fearful of addiction, he always carried benzodiazepines when out of the house "just in case." He had a small circle of friends he had known since high school; most were former members of the baseball team on which he had been a successful player. None of his friends knew about his anxiety struggles, which developed while he was away in college. He initially wanted to be a teacher, but his father had insisted that he should be an engineer and had selected the school, threatening to not pay for college if he went anywhere else. Although he was excellent at it, George did not like engineering. His panic attacks began in his second semester. By force of will he struggled through school as his anxiety problem worsened. By the time he returned home he had a serious anxiety disorder. To hide it from his friends, he constructed an imaginary second life for their consumption, complete with an imaginary engineering consulting job that demanded travel, business meetings at all hours, and other last-minute demands that he then used to explain his absences from social commitments when the anxiety was too great. He rarely had panic attacks in his house, which is where he spent the vast majority of his time, playing his guitar, interacting with others on the Internet, and trying to come up with inventions that might support him. He did not feel that he could leave his father's house because he lived there rent-free. His last date was 3 years ago. He had had two long-term relationships since returning from college. One was with a girl he knew in high school, and the other began through an Internet dating site. Both ended because of his girlfriends' frustration over his restricted lifestyle.

George was not seeking ACT per se when he called asking for help. He was calling because he was referred by a therapist who had done client-focused work with him for 2 years without significant improvement. The course of ACT consisted of one session of assessment, a session on "creative hopelessness" and agreement on a therapeutic contract, 12 primary therapy sessions, and three follow-up sessions in a wind-down period. The sequence of therapy was mixed, but four of the primary therapy sessions focused heavily on acceptance and defusion skills, three sessions primarily focused on values, and three sessions were focused on a mix of psychological flexibility processes and exposure (including one on a local highway and one in a forest about 30 miles away). The follow-up sessions were mixed sessions, with the final session broadly focused on how to deal with relapses. Homework consisted of contemplative-practice audio recordings and, after the midpoint in therapy, regular values-based exposure exercises. Now is not the time to explain the therapy itself—we will do that with the entire book. Rather, we will describe where therapy ended up and show three turning points. Later on in the book you will see more of how the session content we have just listed could have produced such changes.

At the end of therapy, George had left his father's house and moved to a small apartment. He got a temporary job as a shop instructor in a local high school. He no longer used or carried benzodiazepines. He had told his friends about his anxiety problems and was dating a woman he had met in college. He had occasional anxiety attacks, but they no longer led to avoidance and were not experienced as something traumatic. He explained the difference this way:

> Even number 10 anxiety attacks are not the same as panic attacks. They're just anxiety. So what? I used to think that avoiding anxiety was life and death. Now I see it differently—what is life and death is keeping my hands off my anxiety. It can come along for the ride if it wants to. I almost welcome the challenge—I learn something every time Mr. Anxiety shows up.

A year after termination of therapy, George was married and soon had a son. His job became permanent, and he was also a volunteer assistant coach for the high school baseball team.

Three turning points in therapy characterize the nature of the course of the intervention. George initially described his struggle with anxiety in violent terms, calling it "a cage fight to the death." In an early session on emotional acceptance and learning to see his thoughts unfold in the moment (part of what is called *defusion*), he was asked in an eyes-closed *physicalizing exercise* to put his anxiety out in front of him on the floor and to answer questions about its physical form (see Hayes, Strosahl, &

Wilson, 1999, pp. 170–171). George thus described his anxiety as huge, black, quick-moving, powerful, with sharp points covering it, and a sticky, smooth texture inside. When asked what he felt about this object, he said he loathed it. He was asked to put his sense of loathing out in front of him, while still leaving anxiety out there as well. When the physicalizing process was applied to the sense of loathing, it was cream-colored and blob-like. It was slow-moving and slightly slimy on the outside. It was incredibly strong, and on the inside it pulsed like a fist being clenched and unclenched over and over.

Therapist: Can you leave it out there, just for now? We will take it back later. But just for now I want you to see if you can just look at this sense of loathing the way you might look at an object you come across in a room. It's cream-colored, blobby, slimy, slow-moving, strong and pulsing. Is that OK?

George: Yeah. It's OK. It's kind of good to see it in a way. Like I guess I knew it was there but really I've been more focused on anxiety so this is something different.

Therapist: OK. Well let's go look at anxiety now. Glance back over at anxiety. Is it still out there?

George: Yeah.

Therapist: What does it look like?

George: Weird. Completely different. It looks sort of like a pile of fabric. Maybe an old shower curtain. Dirty white. Translucent in places. I'm not sure if it can even move. It's just a heap.

Therapist: And how strong is it?

George: Maybe it could cover something. I wouldn't call that strong.

Therapist: [pause] What does this dirty white pile tell you?

George: [pause] It's my own hate that is feeding it. I'm giving it its power.

This experience marked a turning in the client's approach as he focused more and more on his relationship to anxiety rather than on anxiety itself.

He often used the phrase "So what?" to mean that anxiety was just anxiety and he was not going to feed it by his own avoidance, hate, and struggle.

In the initial session on values, George had denied that he wanted children and claimed that engineering was "OK. It was not what I wanted initially, but it brought in some money." The next week, he reported a transformational experience. While on a walk near his house, he stopped in a small park. A father was playing baseball with his two elementary-school-age sons. Although the children showed limited baseball skills, the father was enthusiastic, encouraging, and obviously having a great time with his kids. As he watched this scene unfold, George found himself crying. He was confused by the experience but sensed that it was important. He sat a bit away from the ball field and watched the family play for a long time, tears slowly running down his cheeks.

His core of treatment opened him up to the idea that he had been chronically avoiding his own wants and desires. He had originally wanted to be a teacher, in part because he wanted to give support and encouragement to children, but had allowed himself to be bullied by his well-meaning but domineering father into another career path not of his choosing. Furthermore, George realized that, far from not wanting children, he wanted to have a loving family more than anything but felt too inadequate to trust his abilities as a father.

Some weeks later, as he became more accepting of his anxiety and his struggles as a result of therapy, he told a friend that he did not actually have a regular job because he had been dealing with an anxiety disorder and had been ashamed to admit it, but that he was now making good progress with it. His friend worked in the local high school and knew of an emergency opening for a shop instructor due to an instructor's moving away mid-semester. The image of wanting to work with kids came to mind, and George immediately said he would apply for the job.

A third turning point occurred during exposure. One of the thoughts that bothered him during panic attacks was that he would get lost and not know where he was. He agreed that a good place to practice acceptance and defusion skills was a forest, so a long therapy session was scheduled there. The therapist went with him but deliberately held back during intervals so he could experience anxiety without the safety of the therapist's immediate physical presence. About half an hour into the session, the client let out a loud roar and ran over a hill and out of sight, returning some minutes later. He described the experience as one of feeling a growing sense of anxiety and a desire to retreat. As he began to struggle with anxiety, he began to watch his thoughts and feelings with a sense of curiosity. Instead of running away, he sensed there was more growth to be had by moving toward them. The fearful thought came to him that he might get lost if he went over the top of a wooded hill, where he could no longer see the way out—so he let out a cry and ran straight up and over the hill. He described the feeling with a half-smile as one of "terrifying liberation" and later used that term for experiences such as taking the job, or calling the girl he knew in college.

In some ways we are all like George. We are confronted with a hill with the unknown on the other side and have to decide whether to go back, stand still, or charge up it. ACT is about empowering people to move ahead.

That same message applies to the present moment. Explaining ACT is also rather like a hill that begs to be seen from the other side. So you know what we need to do: Let's charge up it.

SUMMARY

Psychology, and especially psychotherapy, needs to grapple with why human beings suffer so, and why they so often fail to thrive even amidst plenty. The most common answer is based on syndromes, but that is an approach that came from other fields and has failed to prove itself to be progressive after many decades of effort. ACT has another vision that echoes the early days of behavioral thinking in applied psychology: Develop a greater understanding of basic processes that can be used to parse human complexity in a way that makes successful change more likely. If that could be done, it would in effect provide an alternative to the syndromal approach. ACT is based on a comprehensive basic experimental program in cognition, RFT. It is linked to an inductive strategy of knowledge development called a contextual behavioral science approach, and it has developed a small set of putative processes of change organized around the core concept of psychological flexibility.

2

History

For most students of clinical psychology, acceptance and commitment therapy (ACT) is viewed as a relatively new treatment. In terms of popularity, that's certainly correct. Only a small number of people were aware of the approach before the first book-length description of ACT appeared (Hayes, Strosahl, & Wilson, 1999). Its rapid rise in popularity probably can be dated to the national publicity given to the first popular book on ACT (Hayes & Smith, 2005). Nevertheless, ACT is over 30 years old (Hayes, 1982).

THE ROOTS OF ACT

Why was ACT virtually unknown for so long? Where did it come from? Why does it look the way it does? The development history of ACT answers all of these questions. The roots of ACT can be found in behavior therapy and its collapse into cognitive behavior therapy (CBT), but ACT has carried on from there. As we intimated in the last chapter, the developmental strategy embraced by ACT—a contextual behavioral science approach—emerged from that history.

There is a storytelling quality to any intellectual history, and we want to note that the story we are about to tell is idealized to a degree. This is not in an attempt to deceive—it is just that history as lived is messy, idiosyncratic, accidental, and multifaceted. Decisions originally made intuitively will often only later be understood to have been about something of intellectual importance. History makes sense and assumes order in hindsight, and even then many different stories are possible. In what follows we will not regularly remind you to take this story lightly, because we are telling it with an intellectual purpose in mind: understanding ACT. Given that purpose, it seems acceptable to tell the story as if conclusions reached later were generally known at the earlier time, but students, especially, should not expect their own intellectual path to have the kind of apparent clarity that idealized intellectual histories reveal.

Behavior Therapy

When behavior therapy began in the mid-1960s, research in clinical psychology was very weak. Measures and methods were vague. Typically, outcomes were determined by clinical ratings turned into box scores of relative improvement. Controlled research on psychosocial interventions was limited, and the theoretical landscape was dominated by psychoanalytic and humanistic approaches. In the eyes of the early behavior therapists, this set of features delivered a one–two punch to the disciplinary body of clinical psychology because of weak data (punch number one) and unrestricted theorizing (punch number two). Ouch.

The empirical problem could be solved by better outcome research—but the theoretical problem was perhaps more difficult. A good example is provided by the famous case of Little Hans (Freud, 1928/1955). Freud (1928/1955) suggested that Little Hans fearfully stayed home from school, terrified of the horse-drawn carts outside, because he was sexually attracted to his mother and, as a result, feared castration by his father. Staying home to cuddle was the secret purpose of his school phobia, and his fear of horses with their blinders and big teeth was in actuality a fear of his father, with his glasses and angry intent to remove the small boy's testicles. Freud suggested that a horse going through a gate is similar to feces leaving the anus, a loaded cart is like a pregnant woman, and "the falling horse was not only his dying father but also his mother in childbirth" (p. 128).

If you are not rolling your eyes, early behavior therapists certainly were rolling theirs. It was not that these ideas were impossible—it was that they were improbable in comparison to ideas drawn from a basic learning science, and furthermore they seemed so loosely linked to the features of the case as to be beyond falsification. Ideas drawn from the learning laboratories did not have that same problem. Before becoming afraid of going outside, Little Hans had experienced several horse-related frightening events, including seeing a horse-drawn cart fall over amid the cries and screams of riders. Upon hearing that information, you are probably thinking what the early behavior therapists thought: Perhaps Little Hans avoided going outside because he had a learned fear of horses (Wolpe & Rachman, 1960). Psychologists know something about learned aversion from laboratory science, and it is not wild speculation to suppose that such things can happen in normal human situations. In contrast, the interesting but unrestrained analytic ideas seemed more loosely linked to the facts of the case and much more difficult to test.

The first generation of behavior therapy had two commitments, each understandable given the historical background we have just described. Early behavior therapists believed that (a) theories should be built upon the bedrock of scientifically well-established basic behavioral principles, especially those in learning and the ontogenetic evolution of behavior, and (b) applied technologies should be well specified and subject to rigorous scientific tests (Franks & Wilson, 1974).

These roots of behavior therapy are exactly the roots of ACT. We adopted both of them, and we've never let go of either one, even when much of the field outside of traditional behavior therapy did so. Despite that commitment, ACT is not a traditional behavior therapy approach; ACT takes the view that behavior therapy went too far in casting aside clinically rich issues when it rejected psychoanalytic and humanistic approaches.

Traditional behavior therapy focused on direct, overt behavior change. That is fine so far as it goes, but the rejected analytic and humanistic concepts were often attempts to address fundamental human issues that go beyond specific behavior change. Some of the less empirical wings of psychology wanted to understand what people really want out of life or why it is hard to be human. As vague, untested, or outlandish concepts were rejected, such questions also became relatively unfashionable in behavior therapy. That is a step too far. Freud's analysis of Little Hans, for example, shows a proper concern for such issues as the child's individuation, sexuality, and internalization of models of living. These are important concerns, whether or not theorizing became too unrestrained or untestable, and it was wrong to set such concerns aside. ACT is based on the idea that psychological theories have to do a better job of rising to the challenge of the human condition, in all of its depth, richness, and complexity, and the deeper clinical traditions have done an excellent job of keeping such issues at the forefront.

There are other reasons for ACT's not being the same as traditional behavior therapy, but they cannot be explained until the next major development in the behavior therapy tradition is understood: The rise of CBT. How and why that happened is central to the ACT story.

Cognitive Behavior Therapy

Human beings are a symbolic species. Words and images refer to other events and to themselves in an orderly way. People think, reason, and problem-solve using symbols. If a psychological approach cannot address the problem of human language and cognition systematically, it has a serious limitation.

There were two strands of thinking in traditional behavior therapy—the associationism of stimulus–response (S-R) learning theory, and the selectivism of behavior analysis. Neither of these traditions had a good explanation for language and higher cognition. They claimed they did, of course, but claims become especially hollow when they cannot be put into a rich program of experimentation and innovative clinical practice.

Clinicians soon became acutely aware of the limitations of traditional behavioral ideas about cognition. In the animal laboratory, such a weakness could be accommodated, at least for a time, but not so in the clinic.

The efforts that were made to bring thoughts into behavioral perspectives were often more terminological than substantive (e.g., some called thoughts *covert operants* or *coverants* for short), and as a result they did not help clinicians know what to *do*. Not even a decade into the development of behavior therapy, clinicians such as Aaron Beck, Albert Ellis, Mike Mahoney, Don Meichenbaum, and many others stood up and said, "This is not good enough." They demanded that a systematic approach to cognition be included in evidence-based treatments. Traditional behavior therapists such as Joseph Wolpe complained, loudly and forcefully, that they had already explained cognition. The followers of B. F. Skinner believed that cognition was a legitimate topic but argued that the same contingencies that produced overt behavior produce thoughts and feelings; if true, that meant that no practical advantage would come from analyzing thought or emotion. Their openness to thoughts, on the one hand, was matched with a practical disinterest, on the other. The early developers of CBT disagreed on both accounts, and clinicians voted with their feet. More was needed.

Acknowledging a problem is not the same as solving it, however. Behavioral principles coming out of the animal lab could be readily applied clinically because *those principles referred to things in the environment that could be altered directly to change behavior.* Principles from hard cognitive science were much more difficult to use. Arcane struggles over cognitive architecture (e.g., Is the mind organized in a bottom-up or top-down fashion? Will symbolic, connectionist, or hybrid approaches lead to more progress?) occupied hundreds of laboratories around the world, but they never seemed to result in practical differences for therapists. That is largely true even to this day.

That lack of practical impact might have been partly due to cognitive science laboratories' not being focused on applied matters, but the bigger reason was that the causes of cognitive differences were putatively in the brain, not in the manipulable context that clinicians could change. It is remarkable how few of the principles from hard cognitive science had a notable role in treatment in the early decades of CBT.

Early CBT researchers took an alternative approach. They began asking their clients what they thought or felt, and they categorized these answers into various forms of schemas, cognitive styles, emotions, cognitive errors, and the like. Thoughts might be said to be rational or irrational, for example. In other words, the therapy developers proceeded to clinical theories of cognition.

It was soon established that people who were struggling psychologically tended to think or feel characteristic things: Depressed people make more cognitive errors; anxious people tend to ruminate about past mistakes. Once these patterns were detected and categorized, it was an entirely logical idea to target the negative features directly—after all, behavior therapy itself had shown that directly targeting overt behavior worked, so it was not a huge leap to start directly targeting, say, cognitive errors. Clients were taught to detect these errors, to test them, dispute them, challenge them, and change them. In a spasm of change, CBT quickly took over what had been behavior therapy, and direct cognitive change efforts took center stage. Without a commitment to laboratory-based learning principles, however, CBT gradually became theoretically diverse because a wide variety of clinical theories could be applied to cognitive and emotional domains. Over the next few decades, in many ways CBT became indistinguishable from empirically based clinical interventions writ large. Empirical clinical approaches made enormous strides, but virtually any theory, process, or principle could be part of CBT provided it was linked to an evidence-based treatment.

There is much to be proud of in CBT. Evidence-based treatments were left broader and deeper than ever before, and cognitive, emotional, and overt behavioral domains were all established as legitimate targets of intervention. But something was also being left behind.

CREATING A DISTINCT TRADITION

This brief history of the rise of CBT sets the stage to explain the first of the final two roots of ACT. We agreed that cognition had to be explained and that traditional behavioral accounts were inadequate. But ACT also was based on the idea that it was too risky to build an intervention approach using clinical theories of language and cognition and to abandon the idea of treatment based on well-established laboratory principles. We suspected that traditional CBT had the right problem but the wrong solution. Instead, we wanted to come up with a solution consistent with the best of the behavioral tradition: We needed to develop an augmented set of behavioral principles that included a robust and pragmatically useful behavioral account of human language and cognition itself.

The Philosophy of Science Undergirding ACT

This part of the ACT history requires some understanding also of its philosophical foundation. We doubted that it was useful to think of any psychological activity as the cause of another. The reason for our skepticism was more pragmatic than a matter of what is "real." Thoughts, emotions, and overt actions are all dependent variables in psychology, and the word *cause* says "I've found the answer." An answer that starts and ends with dependent variables cannot be a full answer for a practitioner in a pragmatic sense. Clinicians need independent variables—things they can directly alter to produce reliable outcomes. We believed that any good explanation for cognition and its impact needed to reveal the history and circumstances that led to certain thoughts—*and* the history and circumstances in which particular thoughts, emotions, and actions related to each other or not.

It is the last part that is most unusual. It focuses on the historical and situational contexts in which thoughts have or do not have given functions—which is not surprising, considering that ACT emerged from the wing of behavior analysis that emphasized functional contextual thinking. For example, a person having the thought "I'm bad" might have come by it quite honestly, say, from a critical parent. In a normal frame of mind, this thought might have quite a punch.

There are many situations in which such thoughts do not have much impact, however. Suppose the person thinking "I'm bad" is playing the role of an insecure person with a critical parent in a major movie. In the former case, intense thoughts of that kind might lead to suicidal urges; in the latter case, they might lead to dreams of a Best Actor award.

Traditional cognitive views seemed to be based on elemental realistic assumptions (the term *mechanistic* would apply, but we prefer to avoid its pejorative connotations and use *elemental realistic* instead). In other words, the focus was on discovering and modeling the parts, relations, and forces that explain psychological events.

The early CBT developers seemed to assume that the world is already arranged into discrete parts ("thoughts," "emotions"). These parts are thought to influence each other by their form and arrangements and by the forces that they channel (e.g., given a schema, a trigger leads to a maladaptive thought, which leads to a difficult emotion and thus to an overt behavior). The goal of elemental realism is to model the real world: to understand how these parts, relations, and forces are arranged (Pepper, 1942).

Elemental realism has had a long and relatively successful history in psychology and indeed in much of natural science. It served as the foundation of S-R learning theory and its descendant, information processing. The models that result, however, can present practical problems for clinicians because dependent variables and independent variables can be of equal status in elemental realist models. If we state this in a typical way, you will see what we mean (indeed, you might even agree with it). Suppose we claim that "attitudes are as much a cause of behavior as is the environment." That sounds good, but it contains the idea that there is no requirement that models of the world point to manipulable events. An attitude is a *dependent* variable, and it is the job of psychology to explain attitudes. Behavior is the same. No practitioner knows how to change attitudes or behavior directly. If "attitudes cause behavior," where are the *independent* variables the clinician can directly change? What causes the attitude? And what causes attitudes and behavior to relate as they do? Without answers to these questions, models of what is supposedly "real" can leave clinicians high and dry, practically speaking.

ACT is based on a different philosophical idea called *functional contextualism.* It, too, has a long history (it can be traced back to the father of American psychology, William James, and his brand of pragmatism), but it is less mainstream. Functional contextualists assume that psychological actions are inextricably intertwined with their historical and situational contexts. Actions are grouped by their embedded history and purpose. It is a convenient fiction to treat so-called elements *as* elements because their function is seen only in and with a context.

Let's give an example. Suppose a person raises her hand. If a functional contextualist were asked, "What did she just do?" the proper answers would be "I do not know yet" and "Why do you want to know?"

It is not yet possible to categorize what she did because the same action in a topographical sense could be part of getting attention, stretching, pointing at a bird, expressing happiness, drying out a wet underarm, or scores of other things. In a functional contextual perspective, actions need to be categorized by history and purpose, so *these are all different actions.* If the action is successful, it may reoccur in similar circumstances, but "successful" can mean many different and quite particular things, depending on the purpose of the action.

The analyses of scientists are also always defined by their purpose as well, and thus a second question also has to be asked: "Why do you want to know?" Successful actions accomplish their purposes. For contextualists, the interest is in making a difference—precisely, broadly, and connected to other levels of science. To do that, however, we need to know what kind of difference is intended. Are we trying to change the occurrence of the behavior? Predict when it will happen next? Understand its impact on others? Different goals may dictate different means, and thus the goals of analysis may dictate the form of analysis or how events are chunked. Contextualists have no interest in modeling reality in the abstract, whatever that is. They want to interact with the world in a useful way.

We don't expect a thumbnail description of the philosophy of science underlying ACT to satisfy you. This is an arcane topic that goes far beyond a book of this kind (but you can read more about it in Biglan & Hayes, 1996; Hayes, Hayes, & Reese, 1988; Hayes, Hayes, Reese, & Sarbin, 1993). Suffice it to say that these philosophical differences led us to be interested in the manipulable contextual events that determine how thoughts, feelings, and behavior are related to one another so that these events can be predicted and changed.

Abandoning the Traditional Cognitive Model

When we examined early CBT methods in a series of studies, traditional cognitive ideas consistently failed this functional test. By "traditional cognitive ideas" we mean in particular the idea that *what* people think causes what they feel and do. From our perspective, we were willing to assume that cognition was real, important, and related to emotions and behavior, but we suspected that the nature of that relationship depended on other contextual features (e.g., the social context in therapy, the psychological context of the individual). For example, we found that teaching clients to say more rational things about their fears had positive effects but only if the clients believed that others (e.g., the therapist) knew what they were saying to themselves. The impact of cognitive change methods appeared to be based in part on a kind of social commitment. If people were tricked into thinking that even their therapist did not know the specific positive alternatives that were being said, the interventions had no effect (e.g., see Hayes & Wolf, 1984; Rosenfarb & Hayes 1984; Zettle & Hayes, 1983). As another example, we found that self-monitoring did more than engage self-control processes—it served as a kind of external cue or instruction, reminding people of the consequences of action (Hayes & Nelson, 1983; Nelson & Hayes, 1981). Self-reinforcement worked much the same way (Hayes et al., 1985; Nelson, Hayes, Spong, Jarrett, & McKnight, 1983). We learned that the effects of aggressive models on children's behavior were in part dependent on the consequences of those actions (Hayes, Rincover, & Volosin, 1980). In area after area, when we looked we found that context mattered and could easily trump the importance of the form or the frequency of cognitive events.

Early Work on Rule Governance

An alternative approach to these issues was needed. ACT began to form as we applied a more contextual perspective to the impact of verbal rules. The idea of rule-governed behavior had emerged in behavior analysis, becoming more dominant in research in the late 1970s and the 1980s (for a book-length review, see Hayes, 1989). At the time ACT was developed in preliminary form, we knew that verbal rules could evoke behavior quickly and precisely, but the behavior that resulted was often remarkably insensitive to subsequent changes in context, especially if those changes were hard to detect and were not themselves contained within the rule.

Let's take the simplest of possible examples. Suppose we sit a person down in front of a keyboard and say, "Push this key rapidly to earn money." We arrange for a quarter to drop into a dish every tenth push on average (i.e., sometimes after five pushes, or sometimes after 14, but every 10th on average). After a while, we change that schedule without telling the person—for example, we arrange it so that a quarter drops into the dish following the first push after a variable time delay from the last quarter, say, after 5 seconds (i.e., sometimes the first push after 3 seconds, or 12, and so on but averaging after 5 seconds of delay). Every creature on the planet soon slows down its rate of responding when schedules shift like that. Every creature, that is, but one. Humans generally blast ahead almost indefinitely—as if the schedule had not changed at all. And those who do slow down will likely be able to say why: The payoffs are now based on time, not the rate of pushing the key.

There are many examples of these effects. We were heavily involved in such research (e.g., Hayes, Brownstein, Haas, & Greenway, 1986; Hayes, Brownstein, Zettle, Rosenfarb, & Korn, 1986). One of the bottom-line conclusions was that rules induced a kind of insensitivity to the impact of programmed contingencies (the relationships between action and context) because they linked behavior to *another* contingency stream involved in the production and following of verbal rules, such as doing what you say you will do, doing what others expect, or just being consistent. In a sense, rules narrowed the range of behavior; they could make delayed or occasional consequences more salient, but they often seemed to block out the impact of events outside of the rule, making it more difficult to explore and to learn based on experience (Hayes, Zettle, & Rosenfarb, 1989; Rosenfarb, Hayes, & Linehan, 1989). The resulting patterns looked remarkably like what we were seeing in the clinic.

People who are suffering are usually doing things they think will solve their problems. What they are trying might work in other areas or might have worked in other times, but not here, not now. When problems persist, however, often another variant of the same problem-solving strategy will be tried. Round after round of themes and variations might follow. The "insensitivity" we were seeing in studies of rule governance seemed to provide a general guide to this clinical phenomenon. People were trying "more, different, and better" variants of the same basic strategies and rules without being able to look outside of them. We could see it in our lab; we could see it in our clients; indeed, we could see it in ourselves.

We came to the conclusion that rules can interfere with experiential learning and in that sense make behavior rigid and insensitive to its actual impact (Hayes et al., 1989). Instead of teaching people to abandon the "wrong" rules and adopt the "right" rules, we began to think that therapy needed to create contexts that would help people be more open and flexible. In other words, we thought that people sometimes needed to learn how to be more guided by experience and less guided by rules, whatever their form.

Comprehensive Distancing: Undermining Excessive Rule Control

This idea was a turning point. It led fairly quickly to a set of methods designed to create more distance between the person and his or her own thoughts; to help people learn to feel their emotions more deeply and to learn from them; and to focus on linking behavior to what people really wanted in their lives. The specific interventions came from many places in addition to behavior therapy (e.g., exposure, implosive therapy, response prevention) or cognitive therapy (e.g., distancing), including the human potential movement (e.g., est trainings), gestalt therapy, Eastern psychology, T-groups, George Kelly's fixed-role therapy, and other areas. Once we knew what we wanted to do, coming up with possible methods was not difficult. In the early 1980s, we began testing these early ACT protocols; many of the methods they contained are still used in ACT today. We called the method *comprehensive distancing,* borrowing the term *distancing* from Aaron Beck.

In traditional CBT, distancing is the step of backing up from thoughts enough to see them so that they can be noted, tested, challenged, and changed. We added the word *comprehensive* to describe our idea that if you just backed up from thoughts and watched them unfold without compliance or attachment, you could take what might be useful in them and leave the rest to shaping by actual experience.

We conducted three randomized studies of these methods between 1982 and 1985. Robert Zettle (Steve Hayes's first doctoral student) went to Philadelphia in 1983 to intern with Aaron Beck and did his dissertation there, comparing what would become ACT and Beck's cognitive therapy.

In this small randomized trial, Zettle found that an acceptance-focused approach did better with depressed individuals than did cognitive therapy (Zettle & Hayes, 1986). Furthermore, ACT worked according to a different process—the occurrence of depressogenic thoughts didn't "mediate" (functionally explain) outcomes, but reduced believability of these thoughts did so (mediation analysis was barely known when this study was done, but the formal mediation analysis is reported in Hayes et al., 2006; see also Zettle, Rains, & Hayes, 2011, for a reanalysis of a similar study originally done 3 years later, Zettle & Rains, 1989, that replicated these effects). A laboratory-based pain study found that ACT could do better than the best CBT protocol at the time. (The study was filed away for 15 years, but was eventually published; Hayes, Bissett, et al., 1999). A study of obesity showed that ACT did as well as or better than the best CBT protocol at the time. It was never published, but the methods, refined and successfully tested many years later, focused on the entangling effect of self-stigma and shame and on the need for acceptance of emotions and a focus on values in health-related efforts (Lillis, Hayes, Bunting, & Masuda, 2009).

We are ready to take a breath and summarize where ACT was in the mid-1980s. We based ACT on five key commitments. We wanted

1. to build a model of health, pathology, prevention, and intervention based on the bedrock of scientifically well-established basic behavioral principles, especially those learning principles that describe the ontogenetic evolution of behavior;
2. to create applied methods that were well specified and rigorously tested scientifically, with good internal and especially external validity;
3. to create a model that took seriously the deepest issues in the clinical traditions and in human experience more generally, without any hint of minimization or "explaining away" these issues;
4. to provide an augmented set of principles of behavior change that included a useful and comprehensive behavioral account of human language and cognition; and
5. to focus especially on the conditions in which cognition and emotion relate or do not relate to overt action.

Why So Obscure So Long?

The foregoing explains where ACT came from and a bit about why it looks the way it does. We have yet to explain to you why ACT has been virtually unknown for so long, however. This invisibility is a bit surprising, given that more than 25 years ago we had reason to believe that ACT could make an impact that was as good as or better than the evidence-based alternatives of the time, and through a different and interesting process. The problem was that commitment number 1 had not been accomplished, because commitment number 4 had not been accomplished. No well-elaborated clinical model based on learning principles was possible because there was as yet no comprehensive behavioral account of human language and cognition.

We did have the useful concept of rule-governed behavior, but that was not enough for this reason: We did not really know what a rule was! No one else in the behavioral tradition did either, Skinner included (Hayes, 1989). We could give examples of instructions and rules, of course—but so could our grandmothers. Scientifically speaking, any concept defined entirely by examples is a concept that is not understood. If we rushed ahead and published all our early trials, we would be doing exactly what we originally feared would slow down long-term progress in CBT—namely, that testing treatment methods without understanding their underpinnings in terms of basic behavioral principles could easily lead to dead ends. In the late 1980s we stopped doing randomized controlled trials (RCTs) of ACT and did not resume them until 2002 (Bach & Hayes, 2002). During that long hiatus, we developed a behavioral account of cognition that worked. It was a risky thing to do, but we thought the commitments we listed above were that important.

Relational Frame Theory

The theory we developed is called relational frame theory (RFT; Hayes, Barnes-Holmes, & Roche, 2001). Human beings readily do something that other animals either do not do at all, or do only with enormous difficulty (that part is still being argued): Upon learning that an object is called X, they derive that anything called X is that object; in other words, the learning goes both ways.

Let's consider a simple naming example before exploring how it could have gotten this way. Suppose an English-speaking child who knows only that a ball is called "ball," learns that "ball" is *mpira* in Swahili. Normal children will say "ball" when shown the object—that was directly trained and there is nothing remarkable about it. But they will not only look toward the ball when hearing "ball" (without any additional direct training) but after learning the new word they will also look toward the ball upon hearing "*mpira*," or might even say "*mpira*" when seeing the ball. That is remarkable. You can think of this as a triangle among three events—an object and its two names. If you train any two sides in one direction, you will get all sides in all directions. This is an example of what is called in RFT *derived relational responding*. Even babies have shown derived relational responding of this kind (e.g., Lipkens, Hayes, & Hayes, 1993).

What RFT does is to provide a process account for derived relational responding, and one with important clinical implications. According to RFT, these effects happen because they are learned instrumental actions. What is learned is a pattern of derived relational responding regulated by certain cues—a *relational frame*. Babies do this remarkable thing only if they have some training to do it (Luciano, Gómez-Becerra, & Rodríguez-Valverde, 2007).

Let's stay with naming, because it is one of the earliest occurrences and the training history needed is relatively easy to describe. A young child has hundreds of examples of the same response frame: [object] *is* [oral name]. A ball is "ball"; mama is "mama"; and so on. In all of these specific examples it is also the case that the reverse is true: [verbal name] *is* [object]. That consistency can lead the child to learn not just the specific instance but also the larger relational frame. For example, if the child learns for the first time that a strange object is called a "metronome," then pointing to a metronome when hearing that name is likely to be rewarded. The same is true when the relation is initially learned in the opposite direction. A child who has learned to point toward a dog when hearing "Where is the dog?" will also receive praise if answering "A dog" when shown a dog and asked, "What's this?"

With enough interlinked examples that go in both directions (and cues to indicate that this is such a situation), RFT claims that children learn to derive a network of relations on the basis of small subsets of trained relations. Expressions like "is" or "better than" or "opposite of" become arbitrary contextual cues for *particular* relational frames—those of similarity, comparison, or opposition, for example.

Relational frames probably emerged originally as a simple extension of social cooperation. Humans are by far the most cooperative primates, probably in part because humans are "campfire primates" who evolved in small competing groups (Nowak, Tarnita, & Wilson, 2010). It is worth noting that the simple ability to reverse an object → name or name → object relation affords a reversal of roles in an interchange between a speaker and a listener. This flexibility is not just a cognitive relation, it is also a social one. For a highly social species, developing a form of communication in which symbols apply regardless of role would greatly extend the possibility of cooperation. For example, on learning object → name (a speaker role) normal humans could respond effectively to "get me a [name]" (a listener role). Being able to do that without requiring training in every instance is enormously efficient and would be competitively useful among cooperative bands.

Relational frames are often learned initially with examples that are physically related in particular ways, as when children learn similarity and difference by playing "One of These Things is Not Like the Other" or learn comparative relations by properly sequencing a series of objects of various sizes. Soon enough, however, arbitrary cues become dominant in controlling how events are related, not just the formal appearances of the related events.

Here is an example everyone has seen: Given a choice between a penny, a nickel, and a dime, young children who are just learning that coins can be used to buy things will universally prefer the nickel over the dime or penny. It makes sense. The nickel is biggest and, hence, apparently the most valued. In our imaginary example, let's suppose the child has spent only nickels and has no direct experience of the value of pennies or dimes. As arbitrary cues take over comparative framing, if that child is told that a penny "is smaller than" a nickel and a nickel "is smaller than" a dime, she will begin to prefer the physically smallest coin—the dime. If the nickel is a reinforcer, the dime is now even more of a reinforcer and the penny less, but not because the child has yet had experiences spending either of the other two coins.

The Arbitrary Nature of Cognition

This penny/nickel/dime example shows two key features of derived relational responding. For one thing, relational framing is *arbitrarily applicable.* Many nonhuman animals can learn to respond to the relationship between events when that relationship is defined entirely by the formal properties of the things that are being related. For example, a nonhuman animal might learn to pick the larger of any two objects, but this comparative relation is defined entirely by their relative size. In human beings, derived relational responding is no longer controlled solely by physical properties of related events: It is controlled by relational cues. This was true even of the names *ball* and *mpira* we started with: relational cues such as the word "is" defined the situation as one of naming. Similarly, when the child was told that "a nickel is smaller than a dime," the relation between nickels and dimes was determined not by their actual relative size but by the arbitrary cue "is smaller than." The many different relational frames humans learn are regulated by particular relational cues.

This means that once a relational frame is learned, it can be brought to bear on any event, provided the right relational cues are present. That is why we call them *frames*—like a picture frame, these relational actions can encompass *anything.*

The property of arbitrary applicability is incredibly important in human problem solving and communication, but here we are finally touching upon one of the reasons that language and cognition present enormous challenges to human beings. If a dime can be "smaller than" a nickel, then what is to prevent a client from feeling that even considerable objective success (a good job, a loving spouse, and so on) is "smaller than" what it should have been? Since the relation is arbitrary, no degree of success can ensure that this will not happen. It is hard to come up with animal models for such a thing, but it is an everyday occurrence for human beings who have the cognitive ability to feel inadequate, incompetent, unsuccessful, or unloved almost regardless of their objective situation.

Cognition Changes Functions

The second thing the penny/nickel/dime example shows is that the functions of events in a symbolic network are determined in part by the functions of other events, changed by the relations among them. The child may have learned that nickels are valuable by spending them, but now pennies and dimes have functions too—a penny is less desired, and a dime is more desired. RFT researchers call this phenomenon a *transformation of stimulus functions* (we have been speaking as if this were a thought experiment, but all of these ideas have been shown experimentally in the laboratory with small children, e.g., Berens & Hayes, 2007).

Let's give a couple of examples of transformations of stimulus functions, in part to show how fast they happen. Suppose you learn that lemons are called "gabbas" and that another name for gabbas is "quantrangs." Now imagine cutting through a big juicy quantrang. Imagine bringing it up to your nose and smelling it. Feel its skin. Imagine putting the newly cut quantrang to your mouth and squeezing so hard that you get a large fresh gulp of quantrang juice.

For some of you, your teeth just went on edge. For many, your mouth has more saliva than it did before. Some of you felt the bumps on the skin or smelled the fruit, even though you'd never heard of quantrangs before.

Now let's try an example using a different relation from one of coordination or naming, so that we can distinguish the relational frame idea from commonsense terms that supposedly explain it, like *association*. Imagine that the opposite of the word *good* is *zog*. Now imagine someone you care about stomping up to you and saying loudly "You are zog!" Some of you just subtly flinched, but not because the reactions to "good" transferred to "zog"—quite the opposite. If we build out a network of opposites (e.g., the opposite of zog is zig, the opposite of zig is zak) some would be reinforcers, and some would be punishers, and mere "association" would not explain the pattern.

These examples help show that the functions of events in a symbolic network are determined in part by the functions of other events in the network, transformed by the derived relations among the events. Transformation of stimulus functions is controlled by arbitrary cues that select the particular functions that are evoked by events in relational frames or networks. In the example above, cues referring to touch, smell, taste, and so on evoked different functions. It is important that transformation of stimulus functions be controlled by context; otherwise all of the functions of an event would be available in its name, and people would try to eat the printed word *lemon* or cut it with a knife. That insight was profoundly important for ACT because it provided a cognitive target for intervention: It's not so much what you think as the function thinking plays.

Using the RFT Foundation

This is a thumbnail account, but in the context of our story the development of RFT provided a behaviorally sensible way forward. Framing events relationally is an observed pattern of action. It is not hypothetical; it is not called "mental"; it is not relegated merely to the brain. It emerges as a result of multiple exemplar training. In a word, it is an *operant.* But relational framing has special properties that distinguish it from other kinds of operants. Language and cognition *are* different from other types of human action. The concept of relational framing provided practical clinical targets.

RFT is a large and growing research program in basic behavioral psychology, with over 150 experimental studies linked to the research program (see ACSB, n.d., for a current list). Unlike all other major theories of cognition, RFT was developed with an eye toward its utility in application. Its key features are all matters of history and circumstances; cognitive actions and their functions are controlled by contextual cues established as meaningful on the basis of one's history.

These are the targets of interventions based on RFT. ACT is a key applied area in which the pragmatic utility of RFT has been tested, but it is not the only one. RFT has led to innovative measures of implicit cognition (e.g., Barnes-Holmes, Hayden, Barnes-Holmes, & Stewart, 2008; Barnes-Holmes, Murtagh, Barnes-Holmes, & Stewart, 2010), analyses of sense of self and theory of mind skills (e.g., McHugh, Barnes-Holmes, & Barnes-Holmes, 2007; McHugh, Barnes-Holmes, Barnes-Holmes, Whelan, & Stewart, 2007), methods of assessing intelligence (e.g., O'Toole & Barnes-Holmes, 2009), methods of increasing intelligence (Cassidy, Roche,

& Hayes, 2011), language training (e.g., Rosales & Rehfeldt, 2007; Weil, Hayes, & Capurro, 2011), analyses of metaphorical reasoning (Lipkens & Hayes, 2009; Stewart, Barnes-Holmes, & Roche, 2004), analysis of verbal motivation (Ju & Hayes, 2008), and a variety of other innovations. Although RFT is a behavioral theory, it is also supported by a growing body of cognitive neuroscience evidence (e.g., Barnes-Holmes et al., 2005, 2005) and is beginning to penetrate mainstream cognitive science (De Houwer, 2011).

As we try to show in Chapter 3 of this volume, with the development of RFT we felt that we had the basic principles needed to model treatment processes and to guide further clinical development. ACT researchers began to develop the applied theory needed in such key areas as experiential avoidance (Hayes, Wilson, Gifford, Follette, & Strosahl, 1996). Component studies and experimental psychopathology studies began to appear (e.g., Hayes, Bissett, et al., 1999). As this all began to come together, the modern era of ACT had truly begun. Concepts and theory were finally available to pursue the five commitments listed earlier. It was time to put these ideas forward and to begin outcome research again.

ACT NOW

As the century turned the corner, the first book on ACT appeared (Hayes, Strosahl, & Wilson, 1999), followed in rapid succession by the first book on RFT (Hayes et al., 2001) and the first general-purpose ACT self-help book (Hayes & Smith, 2005). But ACT was hardly alone. ACT was one of the earliest of the acceptance and mindfulness methods in initial development, but not in popularization, and a whole set of methods had begun appearing in CBT based on ideas that were compatible with ACT and very different from the CBT mainstream.

The Rise of Contextual CBT—the "Third Wave"

It has become common to speak of the aforementioned changes in terms of "waves" (Hayes, 2004a) or "generations" (Hayes, 2004b), with behavior therapy and traditional cognitive behavior therapy representing the first two, respectively, and new methods representing the third. Methods emerged from many different corners of clinical work. These include dialectical behavior therapy (DBT; Linehan, 1993), mindfulness-based cognitive therapy (MBCT; Segal, Williams, & Teasdale, 2002), meta-cognitive therapy (Wells, 2000), integrative behavioral couple therapy (Christensen, Jacobson, & Babcock, 1995), functional analytic psychotherapy (Kohlenberg & Tsai, 1991), modern forms of behavioral activation (Martell, Dimidjian, & Herman-Dunn, 2010), and many others (for a recent review, see Hayes, Villatte, Levin, & Hildebrandt, 2011).

Although the set of such methods is very broad, they all seem to focus on the context and function of psychological events, such as thoughts, sensations, or emotions, rather than primarily targeting the content, validity, intensity, or frequency of such events. For example, Segal, Teasdale, and Williams (2004) stated, "Unlike CBT, there is little emphasis in MBCT on changing the content of thoughts; rather, the emphasis is on changing awareness of and relationship to thoughts" (p. 54; see also similar observations by Dimidjian et al., 2006, p. 668; or Wells, 2008, p. 651). For that reason, these so-called Third Wave CBT methods might more descriptively be called *contextual CBT,* as was proposed in the first book on ACT (Hayes, Strosahl, & Wilson, 1999).

In addition to their contextual focus, these methods tend to take a broad transdiagnostic approach in which "there is no fundamental distinction between the therapist and the client at the level of the processes that needs to be learned" (Pierson & Hayes, 2007, p. 225). Because the processes targeted are thought to apply to clients and therapists alike, most of these new methods suggest that practitioners themselves use these methods on themselves: "Perhaps the most important guiding principle of MBCT is the instructor's own personal mindfulness practice" (Dimidjian, Kleiber, & Segal, 2009, p. 316), and "the task of the consultation group members is to apply DBT to one another" (Linehan, 1993, p. 118). It is important to note that these methods are not hostile to any well-established methods in behavior therapy or CBT; rather, the goal is to carry this tradition forward into deeper clinical issues such as spirituality, meaning, sense of self, relationships, emotional deepening, values, and the like.

Even if ACT had become widely known when it was developed in the early 1980s, it seems unlikely it would have been widely used. Traditional CBT was still very much on the ascent at the time, and ACT developers were among a small minority who sensed that problems would eventually arise from traditional clinical theories of cognition (for some of those problems, see Longmore & Worrell, 2007). Although it was not deliberate, the delay was fortuitous. In the context of all of these other emerging methods, some very successful, a great deal of attention came to ACT not as a result of what it specifically claimed but because of the power of the acceptance and mindfulness movement writ large. In the transition to the new century, the center of gravity of evidence-based treatments has moved rapidly in the direction of ACT and the other contextual CBT methods. These methods have proven to be a wave in more ways than one.

The Increased Popularity of ACT

The deliberately long delay in popularization we have described in this chapter was used to build the philosophical and intellectual foundations of ACT, especially in the area of basic processes. In essence, the purpose was to be ready when and if popularity came. In 2005, a group called the Association for Contextual Behavioral Science (ACBS) sprang up to support the development of ACT and RFT. The society is named for the development strategy behind ACT, which is termed a *contextual behavioral science* (CBS) approach. The key features in a CBS approach (Hayes et al., in press; Vilardaga et al., 2009) include clarity about contextual philosophical assumptions, the search for more adequate behavioral principles, the development of clinician-friendly models linked to basic principles, a focus on processes of change, and wide application of the model, among several other features. In the few years since its founding, ACBS has grown from 800 members in 2005 to nearly 4,600 in 2011. There are active chapters in many countries and language communities around the world, including Japan, France, Italy, Australia/New Zealand, The Netherlands/Belgium, the United Kingdom, the Balkans, and Spain. More than half of the members of ACBS are outside of the United States.

As the number of persons knowledgeable about ACT ballooned, research and dissemination advanced quickly. In 1999, when the first ACT book appeared, there were two small controlled clinical studies on ACT, both in depression. By 2011, there were over 50 RCTs or controlled time series studies, with two or more RCTs in depression, stress, the management of psychosis, anxiety, smoking, addiction, prejudice, chronic pain, chronic disease, personality disorders, obsessive–compulsive and related disorders, prevention of mental health problems, weight, and exercise, plus solo studies in several other areas. In 1999, there was one book on ACT; by 2011, there were more than 60 volumes in every imaginable general area, with translations in more than a dozen languages and original volumes in at least eight languages other than English. About half of these books were trade books meant for nonprofessionals. ACT books regularly rose up the list of popular titles in the United States; in 2006, one such book was 20th on the Amazon list, even beating out Harry Potter for a time.

In 1999, ACT was not yet listed as an evidence-based treatment. By 2011, it was listed by Division 12 (Society of Clinical Psychology) of the American Psychological Association and by the National Registry of Evidence-Based Programs and Practices maintained by the U.S. Substance Abuse and Mental Health Services Administration. The U.S. Department of Veterans Affairs included ACT as one of its major evidence-based procedures targeted for dissemination and spent millions of dollars rolling ACT out throughout its system. The CBS strategy reaches beyond mere randomized trials, but these are all still benchmarks of empirical progress.

In 1999, ACT was infrequently presented at major CBT conferences. By 2011, hardly any conferences on CBT occurred around the world without multiple ACT presentations (e.g., examine the convention programs for the Association for Behavioral and Cognitive Therapies, in which ACT has been the most indexed specific form of CBT over the first decade of conventions in this century). Workshops on ACT occur every week in multiple areas around the world, as an examination of http://www.contextualpsychology.org will show. Thousands of practitioners are being trained in ACT worldwide every year.

Intellectual Development

When ACT research began again in earnest after the publication of the first book on ACT in 1999, the model itself was still rather fluid. Elements were there, but they were not systematized. There were only a few RFT studies formally modeling ACT processes, and mediational analyses were few. Only a few measures had been developed. Dissemination was limited. It was not, then, as though we had waited for everything to be finished before doing outcome research; we just wanted a solid foundation.

Over the next decade the psychological flexibility model that encompasses ACT became fairly well developed. ACT is now almost always presented as organized around this concept and the several processes related to it (e.g., see the revision of the original book on ACT: Hayes, Strosahl, & Wilson, 2011). We developed measures in many specific areas and did a set of mediational studies on the functional pathway that determines how ACT has its effects. We will walk you through that pathway in later chapters.

Despite the enormous range of topics that have been addressed by ACT, a relatively small set of processes are targeted. In most ACT studies, they change more in ACT than in control groups, and positive outcomes have been shown to be linked to these changes. Component studies focused on the impact of many ACT procedures ballooned. RFT studies began to appear regularly that were focused on mindfulness, defusion, sense of self, experiential avoidance, and other clinical topics (e.g., Hooper, Saunders, & McHugh, 2010), showing that the link between RFT and ACT is vital and growing.

Criticism, Assimilation, and Community

With its increased popularity, ACT also began to face fairly vigorous criticism. Although some has been conceptual, the vast majority of it has been methodological. This was welcomed by the ACT community—indeed, some of it was deliberately encouraged because there is a tradition of inviting critics and skeptics to present at ACBS conferences. For example, a skeptical empirical review of ACT research was recently presented by a major CBT researcher who had been invited to several ACT conferences specifically to criticize the existing ACT research base (Öst, 2008). Other reviews have also appeared (Hayes, Luoma, Bond, Masuda, & Lillis, 2006; Powers, Vörding, & Emmelkamp, 2009; Pull, 2009; Ruiz, 2010). Although the details varied, they all seemed to agree that ACT produced medium effect sizes between conditions at posttest and medium-to-large effect sizes at follow-up, across a very wide range of clinical problems.

The focus on methodological weaknesses makes sense, given the stage of development of the area and its breadth of application. Many of the early studies were unfunded, small, and preliminary. Some of the areas to which ACT has been applied have rarely received attention before, so coming up with good control conditions and the like was sometimes difficult. When adjusting for funding levels, ACT research is equal in quality to mainstream CBT research on traditional metrics of quality, but it is higher in its measurement of processes of change and mediation (Gaudiano, 2009). Nevertheless, it is clear that we have a long way to go.

At a clinical level at least, the basic ideas behind ACT have been met with rapid assimilation. ACT helped bring mindfulness, acceptance, and values into the mainstream of evidence-based psychosocial treatments. Many, if not most, of the new treatment developments in evidence-based practice in the modern era seem somehow to address some or all of these topics (see Hayes, Villatte, et al., 2011, for a review). This kind of assimilation has a positive benefit: If you choose to study ACT, you can do so now knowing that you are studying processes that are widely viewed to be of importance to empirical clinical psychology writ large, not just for ACT but for many methods.

There is another reason to take ACT seriously, however: It is designed to contact limits quickly. All scientific theories have ultimately been shown to be wrong if enough time goes by, and surely that will happen for ACT as well. The goal isn't to be right forever; it is to move the ball down the field. If theories and methods are well crafted, they can be extended and tested and their limits determined relatively quickly and with greater certainty. That is how science progresses rapidly, and that is a major point of our strategy of scientific development.

SUMMARY

In this chapter on the history of ACT, we have tried to outline the development strategy we are following rather than emphasize specific ideas or clinical methods per se. ACT is committed to a pragmatic, functional, contextual approach that maintains an interest in the deepest clinical issues, as in analytic and humanistic approaches; a commitment to the inductive, basic science, as in behavior analysis; the use of laboratory-based principles in application, as in behavior therapy; the intense focus on cognition characteristic of cognitive therapy; and the commitment to scientific evaluation, as in CBT and evidence-based treatments more generally. It has done that by taking the time to develop philosophical clarity, a basic science program, and a strategy of scientific development, contextual behavioral science. Once that was done, empirical and clinical work on ACT resumed and the approach developed rapidly.

If you feel that the development strategy being followed is sound, then you can study this approach with a personal conviction that it might yield further dividends. For students or young professionals reading this volume, it may well be *your* efforts that will decide how much progress will be made.

3

Theory

The goal of acceptance and commitment therapy (ACT) is the creation of psychological flexibility. The psychological flexibility model underneath ACT emphasizes six specific processes that promote psychopathology and needless human limitation, and six related processes that promote psychological health and human flourishing. These are shown in Figures 3.1 and 3.2, respectively. In this chapter, we describe each of these positive and negative processes and then organize them into larger chunks, ending up with the definition of ACT.

PSYCHOLOGICAL FLEXIBILITY

Psychological flexibility is the process of contacting the present moment fully as a conscious human being and persisting or changing behavior in the service of chosen values. That skill is argued to be composed of the following processes.

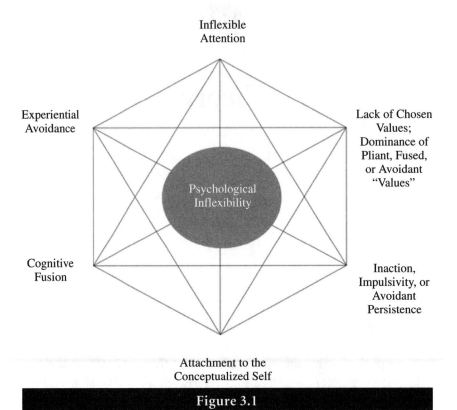

Figure 3.1

The six core processes of psychopathology in the psychological flexibility model that underlies ACT. Copyright 2012 by Steven C. Hayes. Used with permission.

Cognitive Fusion Versus Defusion

In Chapter 2, we described how verbal/cognitive rules can dominate in the regulation of behavior, and we provided a thumbnail relational frame theory (RFT) account of the learned processes that lead to verbal cognitive relations.

If thinking is learned and regulated by arbitrary stimuli, it will always be difficult, if not impossible, to fully eliminate thoughts we do not like. There is no process called unlearning, and it is hard to eliminate all the cues for certain thoughts. Indeed, trying to do so itself creates such cues (Wenzlaff & Wegner, 2000). If a client with obsessive–compulsive disorder tries hard not to think of a disturbing image, for example, the frequency of that image is

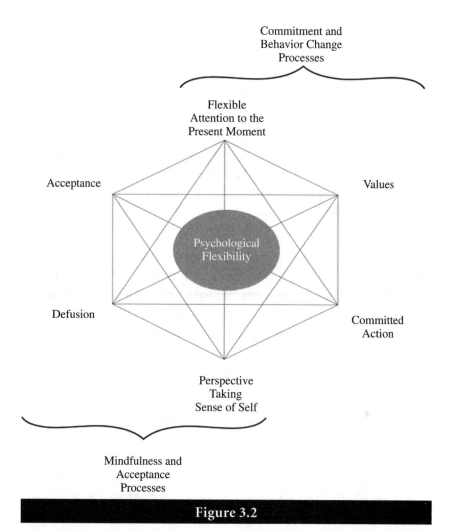

Figure 3.2

The six core processes of intervention and human flourishing in the psychological flexibility model that underlies ACT. Copyright 2012 by Steven C. Hayes. Used with permission.

almost certain to increase, as all of the various distraction cues used become related to the very image being avoided and begin to evoke it.

In RFT, some contextual cues regulate the emergence of relationships between events, but other cues regulate the *functions* of related events. ACT tends to emphasize interventions that change the functional context, not the relational context.

Suppose a person learns that another name for a favorite candy is "jumjaw." Even a single exposure to that training could establish a mutual relation between these two events that may last a lifetime. But that is only half the story. It is possible to undermine the automatic functions of cognitive relations by altering the functional context. We do that in ordinary ways when we, for example, imagine tasting a jumjaw versus looking at one, but this insight from RFT can be used to clinical effect by changing the literal context of thoughts. Suppose a person is struggling with food urges that revolve around the thought "I want a jumjaw." We might diminish the behavioral impact of that thought by saying it aloud in the voice of Donald Duck, or repeating the word jumjaw out loud until it loses all meaning, or noting that "I am having the thought I want a jumjaw." These functional changes are arguably easier and more reliable than the difficult work of changing the occurrence of thoughts. ACT takes advantage of this insight and focuses particularly on the alternation of functional contexts that determine the behavioral impact of verbal/cognitive events.

Cognitive Fusion

Cognitive fusion (or what we will often just call *fusion* for short) is a process in which verbal events have a strong behavioral impact beyond other sources of regulation because they occur in a context of literal meaning. In some external situations, fusion with thought is not harmful to human functioning. A person trying to repair a broken bicycle needs to understand cognitively what is broken and how to fix it; being continuously aware of the process of thinking, in order to increase the psychological distance between the person and his or her thoughts, would likely not add to the effectiveness of this process. Suppose it is clear on inspection that a chain link is damaged. Thinking "I'm having the thought that the chain link is damaged," would be of little help. The chain is damaged. Judgments about why it is damaged will likely help fix it.

That picture changes dramatically when the focus of what is being addressed is not amenable to problem solving. A person who is suffering is not like a bicycle with a broken chain. The emotions and thoughts being struggled with are historical. Some are deeply conditioned, and those aspects of history will not be changed. In such circumstances, ACT practitioners are likely to try to change the *functions* of experiences rather than their occurrence. Cognitive defusion is a classic method of that kind. We will examine this in a somewhat extended example.

Imagine a person who feels insecure, guilt-ridden, and self-critical. Decades earlier, her mother was very demanding and tried to motivate more attention from her daughter by using criticism and blame. A companion DVD to the present volume, also made available by the American Psychological Association (Hayes, 2009), shows a client in exactly that situation. We use other clients as examples in this volume but return to this case most often. We refer to her throughout by the name "Sarah." The transcript entries for Sarah in this volume are edited for clarity, space, and confidentiality, but the actual word-for-word interactions can be seen on the DVD.[1]

Sarah was seen by Steve Hayes in 2008. Sarah is in her early 60s and is returning to therapy. She has chronic health problems due to lung disease. She helps care for her elderly mother, and the relationship is very conflicted. Her mother has always been extremely demanding and critical:

Sarah: Her standards for "if you love me"—well, she has criteria. "If you love me, you'd ____."

Therapist: Right, and then there is a list.

Sarah: And I can do nice things for her, and she notices them, but it's still not enough. You should never say no. You should never say, "I've gotta go." You should always be there to do whatever she wants.

This is not a new pattern. It turns out that even as a young child, Sarah constantly heard, as she put it, "'This should be this and this should

---

[1] The DVD, which can be purchased at http://www.apa.org/pubs/books/, is titled *Acceptance and Commitment Therapy* and is copyrighted by the American Psychological Association. It is important to note that the client's name and other identifying information have been changed here to protect her confidentiality. The reader who watches the DVD may notice some discrepancies.

be that.'" Sarah observes, "It impressed me that my mother was full of 'shoulds.'" The pressure to conform and to serve her mother's needs went all the way up to such judgmental and critical statements as ". . . and you call yourself a Christian."

The result of this history is that it is hard to set reasonable limits without feeling bad about it:

Sarah: I feel bad if I'm not concerned about what my mother needs for her happiness. And so this is kind of painful. I go over here, "But I wanna be a good Christian, I wanna be, you know, good to my mother and love her," but then I'm not responsible for making all of her moments happy. So it feels like a heavy burden.

Therapist: Yeah. Even as you say it, you kind of winced.

Sarah: And even, you know, I got caller ID so I can see when it was her. So that way if I didn't think I could emotionally handle it, I just wouldn't. But even now every time her name comes up on the caller ID, I have *feelings*. I feel overburdened.

Therapist: And sometimes when you don't answer and she's called?

Sarah: You know what? I don't do that so much because I *still* do it to myself. Then I'm thinking, "Oh, what if this time it was something really important?" I've had to deal with a lot of guilt.

Fusion with judgment and self-criticism is extremely painful, but worse than that, it pulls for ineffective actions. Let's apply the same mode of mind to this situation as one might apply to the broken bicycle. The indication that something is broken is the emotional result of the history we have been describing (e.g., "I feel a heavy burden" or "I feel a lot of guilt"). The broken link in the chain is like the negative self-judgment that leads to guilt and an inability to set reasonable limits. This pattern is historical—she was taught to do it. During the session, the client realized how she too often "goes with the shoulds"—directed at herself and her mother. In one of these moments, she declared, "That's scary. The very thing you have hated in someone else, then you start becoming that."

The problem is that, as the person tries to fix the "broken bicycle" of their own history, this very effort can amplify the thoughts and feelings this history produces. It is easy to end up in the paradoxical and unworkable situation of trying judgmentally to eliminate judgment ("I shouldn't say should!"). Difficult thoughts can become even more central. Real behavior change can be put on hold while a war within is fought. Sarah knows this:

Therapist: If you start arguing with them logically, difficult thoughts and feelings can become even more central.

Sarah: I know! Isn't that something?!

In an ACT model, the problem is not automatic thoughts. It's that there is no distance between the person and predictions, judgments, and interpretations. Fusion itself is the problem. Fusion then restricts the ability to be moved by contact with direct experience. This exchange shows the process clearly:

Therapist: And when it's happening, when these thoughts—these "should" thoughts—get going, are they up here, right on you? [therapist holds his hand right in front of his face]. Or are they sort of out there? [therapist holds his hand a couple of feet away from his face].

Sarah: No, they're right up there on me.

Therapist: They're right up on you.

Sarah: Almost like I can't breathe.

Therapist: Almost like you can't . . . Oh, yeah.

Sarah: And when I'm talking to her on the phone like *that* she can be telling me something interesting and I *still* don't wanna talk to her. I mean I don't hate her, but her voice and her mannerisms annoy me.

The effects of fusion as seen in this case are typical. Fusion feeds a problem-solving mode of mind, but treating our inner life that way turns life from a process to be experienced into a problem to be solved.

Defusion

In ACT, therapy itself is viewed as a different context for verbal/cognitive events; the goal is to establish a verbal community that changes how the client *interacts with* or *relates to* thoughts, feelings, and bodily sensations. The main goal is to undermine the excessive literal quality of evaluations and judgments and to relate to them instead as merely aspects of ongoing experience. That is the essence of *defusion*. Exercises, metaphors, and other methods are used to help the client to be able to see that a thought is more like a coffee cup than a lens; that is, it is something one can look *at,* not merely look *from.* In that posture, thoughts need not regulate actions other than mere noticing. They can, if they are helpful, or not, if they are not. The issue is workability toward a goal, not literal "truth."

We give several examples in the next chapter, but let's return to Sarah and show a method for how thoughts can be looked *at,* not *from.*

Therapist: So let's just see if we could sort of take some of that burden off without having to take off the programming. Like, let's just look at how easy it is to get things programmed. If you've got this judgmental critical streak going, sometimes you probably even hear these words in your mother's voice, and I bet you they are so deeply in your head that . . .

Sarah: You're right.

Therapist: Okay, so let's just see how fast it happens. I'm gonna give you three numbers to remember. If you remember them, the people who are doing this filming, they're giving me money, and if you remember them a week from now I'll give you $10,000. Here are the numbers—1, 2, 3. Now if I come back and say, "What are the numbers?" what are you gonna say?

Sarah: The numbers are 1, 2, 3.

Therapist: Oh! Good for you; $10,000. So if I say, "What are the numbers?" you'll say?

Sarah: 1, 2, 3.

Therapist: There's no $10,000. I fibbed. [laughter] If I came back next week, do you suppose you could remember those?

Sarah: I think so.

Therapist: Next month?

Sarah: Probably.

Therapist: It's even possible, possible, next year?

Sarah: Yes.

Therapist: What if a very old man who is bald came up on your deathbed and said, "Sarah, what are the numbers?" Is even that possible?

Sarah: It's possible.

Steven: I've said it twice. Your mother said these judgmental things to you a hundred times.

Sarah: Daily.

Therapist: They will never leave your head. There's no place for them to go. When you're interacting with her, this voice shows up. What are the numbers?

Sarah: 1, 2, 3.

Therapist: And if I get angry with my mother, then I'm . . .

Sarah: Bad. Oh, I see what you are saying! That's why that guilt and judgment just keep coming up!

The What Are the Numbers? exercise is a classic ACT cognitive defusion method. When the person sees how easy it is to program a human mind, conditioned thoughts take on less literal meaning. Having "1, 2, 3" come to mind (perhaps even for life!) means nothing about Sarah other than that she has a history. This is experientially obvious after this exercise. Yet Sarah is taking "I'm bad" literally, as if it means that there is something wrong with her and that something needs to be changed. By metaphorical extension, she now sees that it too could say nothing more about her than that she has a history. In such a moment, the thought "I'm bad" is being looked *at,* not looked *from.*

There are hundreds of specific ACT defusion methods such as the What Are the Numbers? exercise. In this chapter, we have already mentioned word *repletion,* adding "I am having the thought that ___" before difficult thoughts, saying thoughts in unusual voices, or distilling difficult thoughts down to a word and saying it out loud a number of times. The point is not to ridicule thoughts but rather to be able to notice thought as an ongoing process in the moment. Defusion methods can rapidly reduce the believability and distress produced by thoughts. Some well-researched defusion methods are as short as 30 seconds long (e.g., Masuda, Hayes, et al., 2008).

A common objection to our arguments about defusion versus content change in thinking is that if deliberate change or elimination is difficult, unreliable, or risky, traditional cognitive restructuring should not work or should even be harmful. In fact, there is little evidence that cognitive restructuring is an effective component of traditional cognitive behavior therapy (for a review of that evidence, see Longmore & Worrell, 2007). But why isn't it harmful? Some studies suggest that it is (Haeffel, 2010), but we expect it is usually neutral because detecting and trying to change thoughts can do both positive and negative things. It contains an elementary distancing component that arguably has a defusion effect (noticing your thoughts is a key facet of defusion, an argument similar to that being made by mindfulness researchers in cognitive therapy; see Segal, Teasdale, & Williams, 2004). In addition, thinking about how to change thoughts can encourage greater cognitive flexibility just by generating multiple cognitive variants to consider. Indeed, ACT sometimes uses this process by encouraging clients to formulate their self-narrative in several different ways as a defusion method (Hayes, Strosahl, & Wilson, 1999). ACT theory suggests that negative effects from cognitive restructuring would come from consequences such as greater entanglement with difficult thoughts, increased cues for them, greater chance of thought suppression, or amplification of a neurotic self-focus. These unintended effects would vary with the skill of the clinician (skilled cognitive therapists are trained to avoid most of them) and the propensity of individuals to engage in them. Thus, some individuals would benefit, some would be harmed, and on the whole it would be a wash.

EXPERIENTIAL AVOIDANCE VERSUS ACCEPTANCE

All complex living creatures avoid aversive events. The challenge of being human is that, as a result of our own cognitive abilities, we carry aversive events with us at all times and verbal cues alone are enough to recreate them. A dog who is kicked can run from the foot of its owner and feel safer. Where can a person run to avoid a painful memory?

Unable to control pain solely by avoiding painful situations, humans often attempt to avoid negative reactions to painful memories themselves. We numb out, suppress, dissociate, and live more limited and narrow lives so that we won't feel, think, or remember things we don't want to feel, think, or remember. Unfortunately, these methods have costs themselves—and, ironically, can even increase the frequency of the very events we are trying to get rid of.

Experiential avoidance is the attempt to change the form, frequency, or situational sensitivity of experiences even when doing so causes life harm (Hayes et al., 1996). Empirically speaking, experiential avoidance is arguably one of the most toxic adjustment processes known in psychology, contributing to poor outcomes in a wide variety of areas (for recent reviews, see Chawla & Ostafin, 2007; and Hayes, Luoma, Bond, Masuda, & Lillis, 2006).

Despite that poor impact, it is hard to call experiential avoidance abnormal in a statistical sense because it emerges rather naturally in human cognition whenever a normal problem-solving mode of mind is applied to thoughts, feelings, memories, and bodily sensations. A lot of these experiences will be negatively evaluated—pain (betrayal, loss, disappointment, and so on) is a natural part of every human life. It is only a small step from such an evaluation to experiential avoidance.

Experiential avoidance is more likely and especially difficult for those with more painful histories, for those with physiologies that are naturally more prone to arousal or to the ability to relate neutral and aversive events, and for those with family or cultural models of this coping strategy (Chawla & Ostafin, 2007). The modern world is also doing many things that seem to make experiential avoidance more prevalent. The modern media enormously increase the frequency of exposure to pain and horror and yet, at the same time, actively encourage avoidance in order to sell goods and services by conveying the message that the right car, home, clothing, partner, or pill will remove discomfort, sadness, anxiety, or self-doubt.

In ACT, acceptance is taught as an alternative to experiential avoidance or control strategies. Acceptance does not mean tolerance, resignation, fatalism, or putting up with life and its experiences. It means the choice to experience experiences as they are, with awareness, with an attitude of curiosity and openness, and without needless defense. In the context of literal evaluative thought, people want to avoid negative experiences while retaining positive ones. That is not what experiential avoidance does. Suppose, for example, someone very close to you has died. Remembering how loving the person was may bring a smile to your face, but tears will be very close, too, as you realize that, except in memory, you will never experience that particular loving energy again. Thus, if you try to avoid sadness, you will have to avoid not just tears but also appreciation, love, humor at the funny things the person did, and many other experiences. Avoidance tends to go far beyond its target.

Sam is a 20-year-old man who came into therapy following the sudden death of his 46-year-old mother after her short bout with gynecological cancer. He described his situation this way:

Sam: Like I said, I don't know how to grieve. I don't know whether I talk about it, I should cry every time or get all upset. I don't want to get all depressed and have this flood of emotions. I've talked about it so many times that it's almost like I don't even realize I'm talking about it anymore. Sometimes I hardly know who I am. I will be driving along and suddenly think, "Am I driving? Am I even alive?"

From an ACT perspective, this sense of unreality is likely the result of an extreme attempt to avoid. If it is not possible to have the history one has, then the only place to go with that is into a place that is not real.

Ironically, what is likely being avoided is not just tears but also joy, thoughts of death, sadness, laughter, anger, appreciation, and so on. Acceptance is done in ACT in the context of all of the other flexibility processes; it is not some kind of cathartic wallowing in pain. Rather, it is coming into the present in a more open, aware, and curious way. Sam was actually aware of some of this process:

Sam: The biggest thing I am afraid of is becoming overwhelmed like I used to be when I was drunk all the time. I am scared of like having a mental relapse if I open up to the pain of losing my mom. In the past I've been so depressed I can't move; so addicted I can hardly get through a day. So maybe I think that the only way not to go there is just to pretend like everything is OK. But then I don't even feel real.

The initial acceptance work with Sam focused on pain, but, as progress was made there, it opened up other experiences. The clinician asked Sam to walk slowly through the last 3 weeks of his mother's dying. A core memory was especially hard:

Sam: My two brothers and I took turns watching her up in her bedroom. One night she called out because she had to poop and wanted me to get her up. But she was too weak at this point. [pause] I hate this memory. God I hate it. It's traumatic. . . . She was kind of out of her mind at that point, she was on so much medicine she could barely talk. She's like, "I've got to go to the bathroom, son," and I have to say, "Mom just go where you are."

Therapist: Slow this down, Sam. When I hear the word *trauma* I start thinking pain plus "I can't have the pain." You can't remove the pain. And would you want to? Watching your mom die? But we can remove the trauma by withdrawing attachment to the part that says, "I'm not willing to have that pain."

Sam: I don't know quite how to do that.

Therapist: Slow it down. Treat these memories with dignity and care— like holding a dried flower tenderly so you won't damage it.

Sam: [more deliberately] I wasn't ready for this. She went from looking 46 to a few weeks later looking 86. Here I was telling my mom to poop in her diapers. In diapers. She was the rock of the entire family and she was as weak as a baby. I would sit there at night watching her struggle to breathe and pray, "God, would you please just take her."

Therapist: What in there was hardest?

Sam: Seeing her so weak and frail like that and knowing that I can't do anything about it.

As Sam opened up to painful memories, thoughts, and self-judgments, something else started to happen. He saw positive things that were previously hidden.

Therapist: Suppose you had her here now and had just 3 minutes. What would you want to tell her?

Sam: If I had 3 minutes to tell her something?

Therapist: Yeah.

Sam: [pause] I would thank her for everything she did for us.

Therapist: Cool. Very clear.

Sam: [in a quick, matter-of-fact tone] And I'd tell her I love her.

Therapist: You kind of rushed through that one.

Sam: I have trouble telling anybody I love them. I didn't tell my Mom that until a week before she died. [pause, tearing up] I'd say "Mom, I love you. I always will." [pause] And I would say I wish I could have shared more of my life with her. I'm thankful for what she did for me—I see she is with me still.

This is an example of how acceptance gradually opens doors, not just to pain but also to other psychological areas that can be even more difficult to reach, such as love, appreciation, and vulnerability. The goal is not catharsis, and clients are never pushed to go places that are not relevant to current behavior; it is about flexibility.

Conceptualized Self Versus Perspective-Taking Sense of Self

If you ask a person who he is and what he is like, he will typically tell you his life story, personal history, and set of predominant attributes. These often will be woven into a kind of story that explains how he came to be as he is.

This is the conceptualized self: a personal narrative and evaluative description of an individual. When fused with, the conceptualized self is always functionally a lie, even if every element of it is "true," because it claims more than can be known and because it naturally overextends what is known. The vast majority of our personal experiences will never be known or remembered in a cognitively accessible way. This is easily realized if you ask yourself what happened 4 days before your seventh birthday. Follow it with a similar question for the 5th day, 6th day, and so on. On any given day, the vast majority of events are long lost. Furthermore, the relatively small set of moments we do have access to verbally cannot readily be chunked—none of us actually knows in detail how our histories work. That is precisely what psychology is trying to understand, and it has a long way to go; the informal stories we tell ourselves about our lives are hardly scientific.

The problem with the conceptualized self is that it readily becomes a kind of cage. A person attached to a narrative can only move within it. If the current situation is explained by a difficult childhood, it is as if nothing can happen until that childhood changes. If the current situation calls for steps that are outside of a self-narrative, they are doubly hard. If the self-narrative is challenged, the person will likely feel invalidated.

Sam showed some of these features. Although his mother's death called for more emotional openness, he found it difficult because of the self-story that made vulnerability feel weak:

Sam: I have always been a strong-willed person. I don't let things get to me. I kind of feel like everything is my responsibility and like I have to set the example that everything is OK.

In ACT, attachment to the conceptualized self is addressed by promoting contact with a perspective-taking sense of self. There are many names for this part of the model because we are naming that which cannot be named: a transcendent sense of interconnected, boundless consciousness. ACT attempts to create a sense of self in which one experiences consciousness as the arena in which private events occur. It is a context or a perspective from which events can be noticed. In spiritual traditions, this aspect of awareness is termed *big mind* or *one mind* or even considered spirituality itself.

This is one of the areas in which RFT can be most helpful to our understanding because the basic laboratories have made a good deal of progress in demystifying this aspect of consciousness. Perspective taking appears to emerge by learning verbal relations that make sense only with respect to the perspective from which they are viewed, such as up/down, left/right, or we/they, or the three that have been most emphasized empirically: here/there, now/then, and I/you. They are called *deictic relations,* meaning that they have to be learned by demonstration—because only demonstration can include the key feature of perspective taking. For example, if a child is shown "here" as compared to "there" and then runs "there," something strange happens. What was "there" is now "here," and what was "here" is now "there." This makes these relations hard to learn, but when children begin to master them, something else appears: a sense that all events are known from a perspective or point of view of "I/here/now." This becomes the context or perspective for conscious knowledge. It emerges at the same time that children begin to understand that others have a similar sense of perspective, which gives this aspect of consciousness its spatially and temporally extended and socially interconnected qualities. That is why deictic frames are key to theory-of-mind perspective-taking skills (McHugh, Barnes-Holmes, & Barnes-Holmes, 2004), such as understanding deception (McHugh, Barnes-Holmes, Barnes-Holmes, Stewart, & Dymond, 2007) or that others can have false beliefs (McHugh, Barnes-Holmes, Barnes-Holmes, & Stewart, 2006; McHugh, Barnes-Holmes, Barnes-Holmes, Whelan, & Stewart, 2007).

We discuss some ways to do this in the next chapter, but one of the best ways to expand perspective taking is to shift perspectives. This was done repeatedly with Sam. Here are two examples:

Therapist: If your mom could have heard that, what would she think of what she just heard? If you'd actually just take the time to sort of put yourself behind her eyes looking back at you now. What would she say?

Sam: I think she'd tell me that she's really proud of me.

Therapist: If you were 46, the age your mom was, and you could magically look back at yourself right now, what might you want to say about what you're going through right now?

Sam: I'd tell myself I can do this.

Inflexible Attention to the Past and Future Versus Flexible Attention to the Present Moment

In the same way that a conceptualized self is an extension of fusion into issues of self, loss of flexible, intentional contact with the now is an extension of fusion into a process of attention. Rigid attention and failure to come into the present are associated with numerous clinical patterns, such as trauma (Holman & Silver, 1998) and rumination (Davis & Nolen-Hoeksema, 2000).

Contact with the present moment involves attending to what is present in a focused, voluntary, and flexible fashion. Attention is not a resource that is allocated but rather a skill of contacting events in a particular way. If a tiger walked into the room right now, it would likely have an intense impact that crowded out awareness of all other present events. That makes sense in terms of evolution, but it does not make sense when the "tiger" is difficult thoughts or emotions. We do not have a choice of what is in our past, but we do in the present moment, and the present is the past of the future. Consider a person who notices a frightening or worrisome thought. If she acknowledges its presence and then shifts attention to other present events of more importance, a future is being built that will contain fewer past moments needlessly entangled with rumination. As a result, the automatic domination by that thought will continuously lessen. For that to happen in the future, it has to first happen in the present.

Flexible attention to the now is taught by practice. Focusing exercises and guided meditations are used for training. For example, a person may be trained to focus on specific qualities of experience (e.g., bodily sensations, emotions, urges, thoughts). Exercises can narrow or broaden attention (e.g., notice only the sole of one foot, then the soles of both feet). Contemplative practice (e.g., following the breath) provides extended practice in returning to the moment as analytic thought drags attention away, which leads to great skill in attending in a focused, voluntary, and flexible fashion (e.g., Baer, 2003, 2006; Chambers, Chuen Yee Lo, & Allen, 2008; Jha, Krompinger, & Baime, 2007).

This can be done in a simple way just by asking the person to notice what is present. Here is an example from the case of Sam, as he speaks about some of the painful memories associated with his mother's death:

Therapist: Take just a moment just to feel what it feels like to remember that. Just allow that memory to come forward, but as it does, watch what your body does. Watch where you feel it and how you react. What does your body feel like when you remember that moment—what do you feel?

Sam: I feel tense. My neck and shoulders tense.

Therapist: Like you're trying to carry a heavy weight.

Sam: Yeah. It actually literally has caused back and neck problems. Even as I sit here I can feel that tension.

Absent, Compliant, Avoidant, or Fused Values Versus Chosen Values

In ACT, values are chosen consequences of ongoing patterns of behavior that establish positive reinforcers that are present as intrinsic qualities of the behavior itself. If you ask people what they want, they tend to specify goals, not values. Often these goals are feeling states or social results. "I want to be loved" might be an example. This is a result, not a quality of action. "I want to be loving"—choosing to act toward others in a loving way—could be a value.

Furthermore, sometimes people care about things because they have to (fusion), because otherwise they would feel anxiety or guilt (experiential avoidance), or because of simple compliance with the demands of others. None of these is a value in an ACT sense, and none predicts a positive outcome (Sheldon, Ryan, Deci, & Kasser, 2004). Sarah's listing of parental "shoulds" might be an example.

What does predict positive outcomes is the embrace of intrinsic qualities of action, such as choosing to act toward others in a loving way. ACT uses a variety of exercises to help a client choose life directions in various domains (e.g., family, career, spirituality) while undermining verbal processes that might lead to choices based on avoidance, social compliance, or fusion (e.g., "I should value X" or "A good person would value Y" or "My mother wants me to value Z"). Values work is the pragmatic linchpin of ACT. Acceptance, defusion, being present, and so on are not ends in themselves; rather, they clear the path for a more vital, values-consistent life. Life is seen as a process by which valued directions are never fully attained but instead serve to guide the client through a process of vital living.

There are two major ways to explore values: sour and sweet. Deeply moving moments invariably contain within them features of action that are valued. Deeply painful moments contain the same thing: We are hurt in the areas we care about. There is a variety of ACT methods to explore values choices, such as asking the person to write about a particularly meaningful moment and then to reflect on what it suggests about what that person most deeply cares about.

It is also useful for an ACT clinician to listen for values leakage throughout clinical work. Sarah provides an example. Her conflicted relationship with her mother was painful, and, as her pain was discussed, she over and over again leaked what she wanted from herself in her relationships with others. Here are four examples. They are presented in order of their occurrence, with just enough context to suggest what painful situations were being discussed. See if you can notice how values information is embedded in the conversation.

Sarah: I remembered growing up and she would always say, "This should be this" and "This should be that" and one day I remember, I was under 15, I said "Who wrote the Book of Shoulds?" Can't people just be who they want? But you know I didn't realize at that time really what I was saying. But I just—it impressed me that my mother was full of "shoulds" instead of people just being.

***

Sarah: I know thoroughly that I do love her.

Therapist: Yeah. I get that.

Sarah: It's just dealing with her, interacting with her is painful. There's no real connection because she—well, she's quite old now and that could be why. But she's not even aware of who I am.

***

Sarah: I think maybe I feel resentment because I have not been honest with her.

***

Sarah: I just don't start out telling everything. And after I say "I'm fine," that's it. She will talk for an hour without stopping. Everything is about her. Not me, her daughter. It is not "Sarah, what's going on." I don't think my mother even knows me.

What is remarkable is that even after leaking repeatedly (including other examples not listed here) at a critical point in therapy this exchange occurred:

Therapist: Do those thoughts have to change before you could be there with your mother in the way that you want to be there with your mother? Not in the way that the critical voice tells you that you have to be?

Sarah: I guess not . . . but the other thing is I don't even know what I want from my relationship with my mother. It's been so much of that fight with my guilt and shame that I don't even know.

The client is not being deceptive here. The pain → values connection is hidden in exactly the way she describes: Struggling against the pain makes it difficult to slow down and see inside it. In ACT, a kind of flashlight is put on these processes so that values choices can be explored and owned.

Inaction, Impulsivity, or Avoidant Persistence Versus Committed Action

Behavior is the bottom line of living. Nothing in the world of therapy and intervention can be trusted unless or until it appears in the world of behavior. Clients come into therapy with a history of various patterns that undermine successful action, whether those patterns are impulsivity, inaction, or lifeless persistence.

ACT encourages direct changes in behavior that are consistent with the creation of larger and larger patterns of values-based behavior. This is *committed action*, and the commitment is the deliberate creation of behavioral patterns that support the value itself.

In this regard, ACT looks very much like traditional behavior therapy, and almost any behaviorally coherent behavioral change method can be fitted into an ACT protocol, including exposure, skills acquisition, shaping methods, goal setting, and the like. Unlike values, which are constantly instantiated but never achieved as an object, concrete goals that are values consistent can be achieved, and ACT protocols almost always involve therapy work and homework linked to short-, medium-, and long-term behavioral change goals. Behavioral change efforts in turn lead to contact with psychological barriers that are addressed through other ACT processes (e.g., acceptance, defusion). Thus, each of the other five ACT core processes plays a role in facilitating behavioral change.

In the case of Sam, the therapist helps him dig down to a core value, genuineness, and tries to link it to a larger process of building behavioral patterns:

Therapist: It sounds as though you're saying that what's important to you is not just being what society tells you you have to be, but being true to yourself.

Sam: This is very important to me.

Therapist: OK, but when you push these feelings aside, you are not doing that. It would be as if you are driving a car and all of these painful passengers are coming along. But they are your memories, your pain, your thoughts. This is not the culture. This is not society. This is your life. Do you have enough room in that car for all those passengers? And you've still got to drive the car.

Sam: That's a really good metaphor. It is what my life is like.

Therapist: The question life is asking is, "Is it OK to be you, really?" If you can get to that place, then the task is to build it out: "OK, come on, passengers, we're going for a ride." In that posture you've got a pretty powerful place from which you can live your life well with sadness, appreciation, loss, and all the rest coming along with you.

Sam: That's what I am going to try to do. That is what I plan to learn.

In this example, the value of genuineness is first noted and affirmed, and a metaphor is constructed for how this might manifest itself. Learning to carry painful feelings and learning to move ahead toward what is cared about are both aspects of genuineness. Thus, just as driving a car with passengers you'd prefer not to have requires both acceptance of their presence and an eye toward the road, so too being true to oneself involves acceptance of history and an eye toward behavioral choices.

COLLECTIONS OF PSYCHOLOGICAL FLEXIBILITY PROCESSES

Taken as a whole, each of the aforementioned processes supports the other and all target psychological flexibility. The six processes can be chunked. Mindfulness and acceptance processes involve acceptance, defusion, contact with the present moment, and a perspective-taking sense of self. Indeed, these four processes provide a workable behavioral definition of mindfulness (see Fletcher & Hayes, 2005), and the growing body of neurobiological data on mindfulness comports with their importance (Fletcher, Schoendorff, & Hayes, 2010). Commitment and behavior change processes involve contact with the present moment, a perspective-taking sense of self, values, and committed action. Contact with the present moment and issues of transcendence and perspective taking occur in both groupings because we are speaking of conscious human beings in the now in both cases.

You can gather these processes in yet another way. Acceptance and defusion create greater *openness*. A perspective-taking sense of self and flexible contact with the now create greater *awareness*. And values and committed action create more *active engagement*. Contextual cognitive behavior therapy is arguably moving toward these three processes as a consensus model of intervention, because methods that target these three domains are nearly universal across the various new approaches (Hayes, Villatte, et al. 2011).

In Chapter 4, we provide more detail of how ACT is actually done in outpatient psychotherapy. We discuss the role of the therapist, the nature of the therapeutic relationship, and the general therapeutic stance, as well as some of the specific methods.

4

The Therapy Process

In this chapter, we walk through an acceptance and commitment therapy (ACT) approach and show examples of its techniques. Our goal is to provide a broad sense of the substance and feel of ACT. However, a short volume like this is not a substitute for detailed clinical training, so if you are moved to want to learn ACT at a level that will allow you to actually apply it, see "Suggested Readings and Other Materials," which lays out a program.

THE THERAPEUTIC RELATIONSHIP IN ACT

It is common for beginning therapists to believe that therapists must have definitive answers to clients' most important questions. Metaphorically, that vision is vertical: The therapist knows and the client does not.

Most mature psychotherapy approaches suggest backing out of that posture, and ACT does as well. The therapeutic relationship in ACT is based on the psychological flexibility model itself. We seek a relationship that is psychologically open: The thoughts and feelings of the client and the therapist have a place as they are. The relationship is centered and aware; both the client and therapist need to consciously and flexibly attend to their moments together. It is active and engaged as the client and therapist each pursue their values as part of an agreement to develop a working relationship for the good of the client. ACT processes thus are embodied in the relationship.

For that to be done in a flexible way, the therapist also needs to be exploring these same processes within. The therapist does not need to be a personal master of them—a therapist is not in the room as a self-nominated guru—but the therapist has to have a personal commitment to a path of openness, awareness, and engagement.

This kind of relationship is not vertical but horizontal. Both participants are fellow travelers in the journey of life. The therapist may have technical and scientific knowledge in some areas, and a different role, but he or she is able to be helpful in ACT work because of a shared commitment to flexibility processes.

There is a vast literature on the importance of the therapeutic relationship, with some authors even claiming that models and methods add little or nothing beyond that common factor (Wampold, 2001). It is an attractive idea, in a way: Therapists can be confident that they are doing therapy that is "evidence based" just by caring! Unfortunately, it is not so easy. The majority of therapists seem to assume that their therapeutic relationships are above average, but that is statistically impossible unless you live in Lake Wobegone. Therapists need to know *how* to create the kind of relationships that best alter these processes. Common-factor theorists do not provide those key bits of information (and if they do, they are no longer treating the relationship as a common factor—they are then developing a specific therapy approach).

ACT developers have a preliminary answer to why the relationship matters and how it can be produced. We argue that a powerful therapeutic relationship is one that is accepting, active, values based, aware, attentive, and nonjudgmental (Pierson & Hayes, 2007). In other words, a good therapeutic relationship models psychological flexibility and is important in part precisely because it does that. If that idea is correct, and if measures are taken of the therapeutic relationship and of client changes in psychological flexibility, the ability of the therapeutic relationship to account for positive outcomes in ACT should depend on the amount of psychological flexibility it produces in clients. That idea was tested in a recent study with exactly that result: The working alliance mediated follow-up outcomes, but when ACT processes were allowed to compete in a multiple-mediator model, the working alliance no longer contributed significantly to outcomes (Gifford et al., 2011). This does not mean that the therapeutic relationship is unimportant; rather, it suggests that it is important in part because it models, instigates, and supports a more open, aware, and engaged approach to life. That appears to be true in ACT, but we suspect it is true more generally.

The implications for beginning therapists are profound. For one thing, it means that you as a therapist do not have to know everything, as you might in a vertical relationship. Indeed, your fears can become your allies. If you are feeling insecure, confused, or anxious in therapy, be glad; you now have a chance to connect with some of what the client is feeling and to do with yourself what you are asking your client to do. This can humanize the work. Clients see the risks being taken, and they learn from the commitments you make to these processes as a therapist.

A study recently examined beginning therapists with relatively limited training in ACT. As compared with training in other empirically supported treatments, students felt significantly *less* confident in session but produced significantly *better* outcomes (Lappalainen et al., 2007). If you are going to ask a person to open up to experiences and stay focused on values, a place to begin such a journey is right here, with yourself, in your conduct of therapy itself.

ROLE OF THE CLIENT

ACT is client centered. From an ACT perspective, clients are whole and complete persons, possessing everything needed to move ahead and learn. Client values set the course for therapy in ACT, and the changes that need to be made psychologically are more like learning to embrace oneself than like repairing something that is broken.

Clients generally present to therapy beaten and battered by powerful feelings, unpleasant memories, judgments and evaluations from themselves and others, and beliefs about their perceived issues, flaws, deficits, or undesirable qualities. Clients are experiencing psychological pain and typically come to therapy with a logical agenda to make their pain go away, so that they can then start living. The first goal (getting rid of pain) is a *means*, whereas the second goal (living) is an *end*. The problem is that trying to get rid of pain tends to exacerbate it (e.g., Hayes, Luoma, Bond, Masuda, & Lillis, 2006). That paradoxical fact is not just a research finding in the literature on experiential avoidance: It is an experience clients can access directly. The problem is that the culture and human language itself override the client's experience. Instead of being shaped by experience, clients often reach the conclusion that they are at fault or to blame, when in fact they are feeling the results of a kind of cultural oppression.

ACT requires significant, active participation from clients as they step forward: into the present, into their values, into consciousness, into the echoes of their own history. The client is being asked to show up, physically and psychologically, and to engage in therapy as a relationship between two equal human beings.

ROLE OF THE THERAPIST

The primary role of an ACT therapist is to help clients become more fully themselves, with their thoughts and feelings, and to begin to live a more vital life consistent with their values. This is at once an active role, an interactive role, and a personal challenge. Vertical relationships don't ask much of therapists, psychologically speaking, but a horizontal one asks therapists to become more fully themselves, with their thoughts and feelings, and to behave in therapy in a way that is consistent with their values. This is the only place from which a therapist can instigate, model, and support psychological flexibility.

Instigation is the easiest of the three. It contains the many therapeutic interventions that have been developed in ACT: the metaphors, exercises, and methods. How to instigate therapeutic change in ACT is the subject of much of what follows in this chapter.

Instigation cannot work, however, if the therapist is not also modeling ACT processes. If a therapist is trying to instigate greater emotional openness but avoids whenever emotionally difficult issues occur in therapy, clients will often attempt to rescue the clinician at the cost of their own therapy.

This does not mean that ACT therapists need be masters in acceptance, defusion, and so on. Coping models are generally more effective than mastery models anyway because people can see themselves doing these things. Suppose an impasse is reached in therapy, and the client and therapist look at each other awkwardly, not knowing which way to go. An ACT therapist might model defusion and acceptance simply by saying, "I'm sort of at a loss in this moment. I'm having thoughts like, 'It's my job to know what to do,' when in fact I'm not sure as I sit here exactly what to do." Noticing and calling out parallel processes can be a helpful way to engage the client and humanize the work of therapy. ACT asks therapists to walk with their clients, leaning into difficult thoughts, memories, and feelings. Because of this, trainees are encouraged to learn ACT through experiential training in addition to readings and to practice engaging in ACT processes (e.g., acceptance, mindfulness, values) in their daily lives. Often this may include formal contemplative practice as well.

Supporting flexibility processes means being able to read steps forward and reacting in a genuine and positive way when they occur. In a successful course of ACT, the client will begin to abandon avoidance-based agendas and create new patterns of behavior connected to values, bolstered by mindfulness, acceptance, defusion, and a transcendent sense of self. New behavior can be fragile, and if the therapist is not paying keen attention it can actually get in the way of improvements. For example, a client who expresses frustration with the therapist may be opening up to feelings of frustration in a healthy way, perhaps for the first time. If the therapist fails to read the progress and mindlessly becomes defensive, an opportunity to support growth may be missed. Reading steps forward relies not merely on the content of what the client is saying but also on its role in the therapeutic relationship and its deeper functional meaning. Tracking processes on multiple levels for both therapist and client can be difficult, but fortunately the model underlying ACT provides guidance: If the therapist becomes more open, aware, and engaged, making these reads and supporting progress become intuitive. The best way to support acceptance is to be accepting; the best way to support defusion is be defused; and so on.

INFORMED CONSENT

The goal of informed consent is to help the client understand the course of therapy so that he or she can make an informed choice. Although the structure of therapy, the empirical support for ACT, and the available alternatives can be described literally, the core of the work cannot, because ACT is seeking a change in the mode of mind brought to pain and suffering. In a sense, ACT seeks to change how "understanding" works and what it looks like. The solution to this challenge to informed consent is to provide understanding in a more experiential sense. This is typically done through metaphors:

Therapist: It sounds kind of like you've been living inside an ongoing war within, and meanwhile life has become less and less livable. Does it feel like that?

Client: 24/7.

Therapist: See if this seems right: What you've been trying to do is win this war with your anxieties, with your sadness, with your depression, with your urges.

Client: It feels almost life and death.

Therapist: But meanwhile life has become unlivable. A war zone is not a very good place to create a life worth living. Plus, despite all this struggle, it doesn't seem as though this war is being won. Is that fair?

Client: That's why I came to see you.

Therapist: I wonder if your gut sense tells you it is time to explore a different alternative. Suppose we could put down the weapons and walk to the side of the battlefield and start focusing on living, now. The war may still go on. We can still see it. We're just not inside it, invested in the outcome. We've got other things to do. If we work together, this course of therapy will be more like that.

If the client chooses to go in this direction, typically there is an agreement about when an assessment of progress will be made and a warning about therapeutic ups and downs. For example,

> This is kind of like cleaning out a glass that has a lot of mud in it. Things may look like they're getting dirtier as part of the process of clearing up. You will ultimately decide if we are making progress, but meanwhile, even if things look cloudy, we will stick to the course.

If measures of experiential avoidance have been taken and the scores are high, this is also a good time to predict avoidance in therapy itself. A short bit of ACT-based psychoeducation can considerably reduce dropout:

> And based on that questionnaire score I would expect if we start to touch what has been going on, part of you will want to zone out, or skip a session, or even drop out. Instead, those are precisely the times to come in and engage.

CASE CONCEPTUALIZATION

Psychological flexibility is the primary target in ACT. Imagine, for example, that a client is presenting with depressive symptoms, such as feeling sad, having thoughts such as "I am worthless," and withdrawing from others. ACT would not directly target reduction of the frequency or intensity of sadness or "worthlessness" but, rather, would target the client's relationship with these thoughts and feelings, and his or her willingness to engage in values-based behaviors. A successful client would have a great capacity to feel feelings, think thoughts, and still engage in meaningful actions in domains such as work, relationships, and play. To develop a case conceptualization, we look for the strengths in each of the flexibility processes, their history, and how psychological barriers are inhibiting successful values-based action. The goal is to have not just a historical understanding but also a current plan that will build on the client's strengths in order to create more flexibility in difficult areas.

A good place to start is by assessing what is important in the client's life and what kinds of behaviors the client would be engaging in if the presenting problem were not an issue. The goal is to uncover some initial values and goals on which to build a therapeutic contract or treatment agreement. Assessment of the client's presenting problem should give specific attention to where and how the client gets "stuck" in life. In ACT this typically involves identifying the avoidant or fused ways that cognitive and emotional barriers are being addressed. As therapist, you want to know about problematic or aversive thoughts ("I'm a failure . . . worthless . . . unlovable . . . broken"), feelings (sadness, anxiety, shame, anger), memories (past hurts or trauma), or bodily sensations that prompt avoidant or rigid behavioral patterns in the client.

The next step is to identify client strategies and behavioral patterns aimed at reducing or avoiding the unwanted cognitive and emotional experiences identified previously. In other words, what does the client do to try to *not* think or feel a certain way, or experience a certain thing? Examples include avoiding situations or places, using substances to "numb," isolation, displays of anger, closing off emotionally to others, overeating, not eating, self-harm, rituals, and so on. These patterns of behavior will be targeted in therapy.

The key to conceptualizing avoidant or rigid behaviors is to understand them functionally. In other words, what is the behavior in the service of? For example, people with crippling feelings of inadequacy may try to sleep with everyone they meet in an attempt to counteract feeling unlovable or worthless. But a different kind of person with similar feelings of inadequacy may avoid trying to interact with people altogether, in an attempt to defend against feelings of failure and confirmation of worthlessness should attempts to engage others go poorly. In both cases the *functions* of the behaviors are similar, even though their forms are much different.

Similarly, the same behavior might have different functions. For example, one client might seek a new job, which could reflect a process of coming into touch with values (she wants to finally perform work she feels is important) and making room for barriers (fears of failure). A different client might seek new jobs as a chronic pattern of avoidance, choosing to "start over" every time he runs into challenges or resistance, resulting in values conflicts (providing for family, working on inter-personal relationships).

Throughout therapy, you should pay particular attention to nonverbal behavior. Clients can give subtle cues about their stance with regard to difficult life events and associated cognitive and emotional experiences in the form of reduced eye contact, shifting posture, tone of voice, hand clenching, and the like. It can be helpful to ask a client to show in physical form the posture he takes when struggling, avoiding, or being open; some of these same mannerisms will occur naturally in session. Observing physical patterns of avoidance or openness in "real time" throughout therapy can provide useful guides.

A final important consideration for case conceptualization is to assess the cost of avoidant behavioral patterns. We often do this in the context of client-stated values. For example, isolating oneself socially may or may not have a cost to a particular client. If a client values close friendships and wants satisfying family and intimate relationships, isolation has a clear cost. Another client may not value relationships as highly, and thus it may be helpful to focus on other patterns of behavior that do have a high cost for him or her. This "cost" is usually an effective way to get an initial agreement from a client to try difficult or new behaviors in and out of therapy.

Let's apply this to the case of Sarah to see how the hexagonal model of psychological inflexibility and its correction (see Figures 3.1 and 3.2) can guide case conceptualization. As seen in the transcript sections, her mother had been very critical of her as a child. Despite her own health problems, it is hard for her to set limits on her mother's demands. Instead Sarah "goes with the shoulds," using rationalization to suppress her frustration with the relationship. She does this to such a degree that she is not even sure what she wants from her relationship with her mother, even though we can see in the transcript that the values she wants to embrace are seeping out: She wants a genuine, caring, accepting relationship.

The dominance of shoulds, storytelling, and explaining, combined with her critical parental history, suggested that cognitive fusion was the key problem. Her values and ability to take action (e.g., in rising to her own health challenges) were strengths. Thus, the plan was to use defusion methods to create some initial openness and to take advantage of any opening by linking her values to the creation of greater acceptance and openness. From there, setting healthy limits would be psychologically possible. A few additional transcript sections from Sarah in this chapter will show how that plan turned out (with other cases mixed in to show the key therapy processes).

CREATING AN ACT CONTRACT

All therapy requires an agreement between client and therapist about the course of therapy and its larger goal or purpose. In ACT this agreement or *therapeutic contract* typically consists of two goals: learning to deal with experiences in a different way and moving toward values. ACT therapists typically ask for a commitment regarding number of sessions (six to 10 is common in flexible outpatient settings, as is whatever minimum the client can or is allowed to commit to within his or her system of care) and warn that trying to deal with experiences in a different way can be difficult and that it is possible that therapy might not seem to be going in the right direction for the first few sessions.

Most therapies implicitly or explicitly target the content of difficult thoughts and feelings as the focus of assessment and intervention. This agenda is in the name of treatments (e.g., anxiety management) and disorders (e.g., mood disorders). These create mischief for ACT, so the safer process is to validate the history that led to difficult thoughts and feelings (e.g., "Given that kind of childhood circumstance I can see how anxiety would show up") and point to the client's experience of how barriers tend to build out pain (e.g., ". . . but it sounds as though you are saying that the more you fought with it, the worse it has gotten") and how life has been put on hold (e.g., ". . . and meanwhile it seems that your life is getting smaller, less connected with others, less vital. Am I hearing it right?"). Then the two-part ACT contract can be put into play (e.g., "So we are going to need to do two things: one, find another way to relate to that anxiety that does not increase its role in your life and, two, put what you really want in life back on the table, front and center").

STRATEGIES AND TECHNIQUES

In the sections that follow, we walk you through a set of ACT methods. ACT is not linear, but books are, so be aware that any of these processes can occur in any order.

Accepting Where You Are ("Creative Hopelessness")

The client's experience is the guide to what works and what doesn't. In the initial phase of treatment we explore the consequences of behavioral patterns linked to the most common client agenda: "Make the pain stop so I can start living." It is not our role to decide whether or how this agenda works, but it is our role to explore the consequences it has had for the client, based on the client's own experience.

We use initial client complaints to ask about larger patterns. Client problems are typically framed in terms of something the client thinks, feels, remembers, or senses. Relationship or social problems can be an exception, but further exploration often shows this same process in other forms (e.g., "My husband makes me mad when he ____"; "I can't stand it when my wife gets so angry that she _____").

Clients often come into therapy saying "I don't feel good" or "I don't like what I think" or "I don't like what I remember" or "I'm anxious, depressed, a failure." The simple question "What have you done to try to solve that problem?" will lead quickly to the client's problem-solving attempts or, rather, the client's attempts to change or get rid of unwanted thoughts, feelings, memories, or bodily sensations. The second question, "And so how has that worked for you?" will generally lead either to admissions of failure or to partial claims of success. It hasn't worked, or it has worked a little, or for a while. If questions about "working" are expanded, however, usually a list of unworkable solutions expands. Here is an example of an exchange with a client complaining of anxiety:

Client: Well, I've tried benzodiazepines.

Therapist: How did that work?

Client: I felt better. Especially at first. It was a relief.

Therapist: And as you've gone along what has happened? Has this problem that you've been struggling with gotten smaller or bigger? Has it got into more areas of your life?

Client: Well, it's gotten bigger, and yes, it is in more areas now. And now I'm concerned whether or not I'm carrying the pills, if they will work fast enough, if I can get out of the situation enough to take them.

Therapist: So it sounds like this looked like it had some benefit for you especially over the short term. But would it be fair to say that your experience is telling you that this is not really solving the problem? In fact, who knows why, but the problem is actually getting bigger. So what else have you done to get the anxiety to go away?

We usually continue with this kind of questioning, noting what other strategies this client has tried and trying to get an understanding of whether the client's experience tells him that these strategies are working in the long term and making the problems smaller, or whether they are creating larger patterns of ineffective behavior and amplifying the situation. The questions are gradually worded in a way to draw out commonalities in the emotional or cognitive change strategies (e.g., "get the anxiety to go away"). There would be no reason to be in therapy if current problem-solving attempts were actually working in the larger sense of these questions, but clients typically fail to see the implications of their own experience. They don't see the "bigger picture" because they come into therapy in a problem-solving mode of mind, and the "stuckness" they are experiencing comes from applying problem-solving to an area where it does not belong (one's own historically produced thoughts and feelings). Despite that evidence-based assumption, it is important to draw out client experiences that can be used to guide therapy, rather than trying to force an experience on the client.

Paraphrasing and summarizing can be an important tool here, for example:

Therapist: So in trying to control that fear it seems like one of the things that you've done is you've tried avoid situations, and it sounds like although you feel better when you avoid that situation and thus feel less fearful, in the long run it seems as though it's actually getting a little bigger, that you are having to avoid more, and that avoiding is getting in the way of living. Am I reading it right?

A client's identification with this pattern of behavior, although not necessary in order to do ACT, can be a very powerful place from which to start ACT. For example:

Therapist: If that is the case, your biggest ally is your sense that this is not working, because your mind is still going to give you the scary thing of, "If I were to stop trying to control my anxiety, I'm going to be crushed by it." Right? So in a way your hard-earned pain is what we have to stay with here. Your own experience is telling you something, and more of the same is not likely to be helpful. Let's see if we can find a place that's not "bucking up," "smiling through it all," or just "being stronger," but is instead something truly different.

The concept of getting clients in touch with the long-term consequences of behavior is called *workability.* No single behavior is either good or bad but, rather, occurs in a context of what the client values and desires in his or her life. Behaviors are, therefore, either helpful or unhelpful in achieving valued ends. Experiential avoidance is identified as a common target in ACT not because it is harmful each and every time it occurs but because when it is overextended and habitual it tends to get in the way of living a valued life over the long run. The client's experience is the criterion. The test is workability.

A commonly used ACT metaphor for summarizing creative hopelessness and transitioning into other methods is the "tug-of-war metaphor":

Therapist: Maybe it's like you've sort of been in a tug-of-war with this big scary creature, this anxiety monster. In between you and that monster it's like there's a bottomless pit. You've been pulling and pulling and pulling, and the harder you pull the harder that monster pulls back, and it looks like if you lose you're just going to fall into oblivion. Consider the possibility that what we need to do here is something that your logical mind has a hard time with. Our job is not to win this tug-of-war. Our job is to learn how to drop this rope.

With a client who has a minor problem, it might be appropriate to do creative hopelessness in a lighter way. This can be less emotionally challenging and perhaps a bit more like psychoeducation. An example is provided in the case of Sam:

Therapist: Do you think it's working for you to simply try to push away the sadness like that?

Sam: No. It's not working.

Therapist: OK. Because sometimes people try to make these things work for a long period of time, things that aren't working. Maybe your history with addiction and so on has given you some wisdom. Are you pretty clear, like at this level [points to his gut], that not only hasn't it worked, but it's not going to.

Sam: Yeah. I'm done. I don't know what else to do, though. That's why I'm here.

Therapist: OK. That's perfect, because as long as you buy into what your mind starts giving you—"Well, maybe you could just be strong enough and it will go away"—well, then, why do anything other than just try more of that? But if you kind of know that you've got something new to do and that you just don't know how, then we are ready to work.

Beginning ACT therapists often fear that creative hopelessness would make clients want to drop out faster, as opposed to preventing dropout. In our experience, that does not seem to happen. Clients commonly experience a sense of being validated, because, after all, they have worked really hard, and what you are telling them is essentially, "It's not your fault—this is a rigged game. You have some hard-won knowledge as a result and a chance to do something truly different."

However, the time required for creative hopelessness is highly variable. Some clients (sometimes those with the most distress) appreciate the futility of their experiential control efforts very quickly. In other cases, it takes more time for this to sink in. Beginning therapists sometimes try to rush this process, often because of their own discomfort with sitting with the client's sense of distress and hopelessness.

Control Is the Problem

Imagine you were strapped to a chair above a shark tank with the world's most sensitive arousal detector, and you are told that all you have to do is stay completely relaxed, completely calm, and if the detector registers any arousal in you, the seat will go out like a dunking tank at a carnival and you will be plunged into the water with the sharks. It is pretty obvious what would happen, no?

We do this to ourselves metaphorically all the time—try to threaten and force ourselves to think or feel a certain way. Deliberate attempts to control or change unwanted thoughts, feelings, memories, and sensory experiences can in fact cause more suffering in our lives and often does, particularly when we take the stance that we must have or not have a certain experience in order to engage in behavior that is vital and connected to our values. ACT refers to this as "control is the problem." Here is an example of how these issues are raised in ACT:

Therapist: Maybe what's going on here is that conscious, deliberate, purposeful control has been brought into a place where it doesn't belong. What was taking benzodiazapines about?

Client: To get the anxiety to go away.

Therapist: Or else . . . ?

Client: Or else my life would continue to slip away from me. I'm not in control of the most basic aspects of my life.

Therapist: And how do you feel when you think, "I'm not in control of the most basic aspects of my life"?

Client: Anxious as hell.

Therapist: So it all notches up one more notch. In an attempt to avoid this feeling, your life got narrower, and you ended up with even more of this feeling. Do you see what I mean when I say that maybe this is a case of bringing control to a place where it doesn't belong? Maybe life is telling you something: Try to control your feelings and thoughts and you lose control of your life.

Trying to control is built into the problem-solving functions of human cognition. Our minds evolved to categorize, predict, evaluate, and judge. It is how we solve problems verbally, and it has enabled a weak, slow species to take over the planet. The problem is that when these abilities are applied within, our own history is our own enemy, and a human life becomes a problem to be solved instead of a process to be experienced. Despite the unworkability of this approach, we are all given sociocultural messages that we can and should be able to control our thoughts and feelings. At some point in your life you may have been told to "stop crying or I'll give you something to cry about," or "don't think about that," or "there's nothing here to be afraid of now, cut it out." The invalidating message we get early on is that it is not OK to feel what we feel. Even as children it was supposedly our job to feel something different. We never learned quite how, but we did learn to be quiet.

To illustrate the control agenda, you might want to ask clients to keep a daily record of how much they are hurting, feelings of anxiety or depression, or whatever they identify as the problem. Then they would be asked to record how much effort or struggle they put into controlling that, and, finally, how workable that day was overall, meaning that they would ask themselves, "If every day were like today, would my life be moving forward and toward the life I want, or backward and away from it?" Clients typically notice that there's more correlation between struggle and the lack of workability than there is between pain and the lack of workability.

It is important to note that the transition to workability and the introduction of ACT processes (particularly defusion and acceptance) should be done thoughtfully and compassionately. Client struggles are not to be trivialized. A good metric is to ask yourself, "Am I honoring the client's struggle?" If the answer is yes, then you are less likely to invalidate the client.

Defusion

Have you ever had the thought deep down that you're a horrible person or there is something really wrong with you? Perhaps you came by that thought honestly; maybe somebody told you that, your dad screamed it at you, or you derived it on the basis of painful and traumatic events in your life. It is possible that this thought will be with you from time to time for the rest of your life, at times powerfully so, and could be triggered by just about anything that happens to you. Trying to get it out of your mind means you have to focus on it. It means you have to treat it as important. As you do so, you make it more central, you connect it to more events, and you devote more life moments to it. As a result, you might actually make it more frequent, amplifying its impact on your behavior. Treating thoughts literally is called *cognitive fusion,* and it is a primary target of ACT.

Imagine being in a place where you can have whatever thoughts you have, more as you might watch the dialogue in a movie or a play. You can have the thought, "There's something wrong with me," and, without having to change or get rid of it, you can determine its impact on your life. As you experience that thought with perspective, awareness, and curiosity, that is what you are doing. That is the goal of defusion work.

Fusion is so pervasive that the signs of it are often hard to notice. There may be a loss of your sense of being present, like in a daydream; a sense of being caught up in your thoughts, as though your mind were working overtime; a sense of busyness, comparison, and evaluation. Maybe you're often looking to the future or thinking about the past, as opposed to being connected to the now; there may be a sense of struggling to clarify things. Conversely, defusion contains a sense of lightness, flexibility, presence, consciousness, and playfulness. There is a sense that you have the freedom to direct your behavior without the dominance of certain thoughts. Defusion is simply seeing your thoughts as thoughts, so that what you do is determined more by your choices and less by automatic language processes.

In the subsections that follow, we discuss five examples of cognitive fusion processes and techniques designed to address these processes in an attempt to change the context in which thoughts occur. There are hundreds of defusion methods in the ACT literature—these are just a few examples.

Ubiquity

Thoughts are ubiquitous; they are always hanging around. Sometimes they are big or small, loud or soft, good or bad, scary, happy, strange, and so on. But they are there, and they often pull us out of the present moment. It can be useful to simply call this process out and get it in the room. You might consider naming your mind and the mind of your client, noting that there are "four of us" in the room. Or you might refer to the mind as a "word-generating machine" that is constantly churning out thoughts, commenting on everything, judging, having opinions, causing a ruckus. The natural tendency is to look at the world from our thoughts. Defusion allows us to look *at* our thoughts rather than *from* them.

Watching your thoughts without involvement is inherently defusing. Many mindfulness exercises fit the bill. The Thoughts on Clouds exercise is an example:

> I'd like you to close your eyes and simply follow the sound of my voice. Try to focus your attention on your breathing, and notice as each breath enters and exits your nose or mouth. . . . And now I want you to imagine sitting in a lush field . . . Notice the trees and foliage, see the blue sky, try to become aware of your surroundings and really see yourself there . . . And now I want you to lie down and look up to the sky and notice that there are clouds moving at a steady pace across the sky . . . See if you can focus your attention on your thoughts, and as you become aware of a thought, put it on a cloud and watch it float across the sky. . . . Try to put each thought you have on a cloud and watch it as it goes by . . . If you notice that you are no longer viewing the clouds from afar, but rather are caught up in a thought, gently bring yourself back to the field, lying down, gazing up at the clouds, and put each thought, one by one, on a cloud.

When you debrief this exercise, it is a good idea to check in with the client about his or her general experiences first. If the client was unable to perform the exercise, some more basic mindfulness training might be needed (see the Mindfulness section in this chapter). Assuming the client was able to follow the exercise, you might want to discuss the experience of watching thoughts versus being caught up in thoughts. Typically clients are able to watch their thoughts for a while but then get caught up in a sticky thought (something personal or with emotional valence), or a process thought (e.g., "Am I doing this right?"), or perhaps worries about the future or past. This distinction is key because you are trying to teach the client to be able to notice the process of thinking. Nobody is able to do this all the time, nor would that be desirable; rather, it is important to be able to catch oneself entangled in thought, so that fusion or defusion can be used on a basis of workability rather than automaticity.

Literality

Swimming in a stream of thoughts, as we often do, we tend to experience our thoughts as being literally true. ACT calls this the *context of literality*, and it can contribute greatly to suffering. We become like a person so lost in a movie that the threats to the characters seem like personal threats: each sudden sound eliciting a startle, each creak on the stairs evoking an urge to flee. We are like that with our mental sounds and creaks because we've forgotten that they are in large part echoes of moments gone by.

If we treat thoughts as literal, then we must be invested in their content. For example, if you have the thought "I am a horrible person," and you take that thought to be literally true, then it makes sense that you would do anything to try and not have that thought or change that thought in some way to make it possible for you to exist in the world and not be a horrible person. However, if you can step back from the screen and notice that there is a "you" and there is also a thought, maybe there is some room there for you to just have that thought as it is, without struggle.

ACT uses a variety of techniques to undermine the literality of thoughts. For example, clients might be asked to imagine that their negative thoughts (e.g., "I'm a failure," "I can't do anything right") are like a radio station that can't be shut off—it's bad news radio, all bad news all the time! They can also imagine a barrage of negative thoughts as pop-up ads from hell. They can't get a spam blocker for these! Another method is to have clients say their thoughts in silly voices, or say them very slow or very fast, or in the voice of themselves as children. Thoughts can be distilled into a single word and said rapidly aloud for 20 to 30 seconds.

It is important not to use these methods to ridicule thoughts. You can explain it to the client like this:

> When you start seeing thoughts the way you would see things like a billboard or a pop-up ad or radio voice, or when you change how you interact with thoughts by speaking them slowly or singing them, or having a puppet say it to you, it gives you just a little space to look at them and use what is useful in them. It's like stepping away from the computer screen. Then maybe this thought is also just a thought, and not necessarily anything that you have to do anything about, and certainly not something that you have to turn over your life to.

Automaticity

Say whatever words come to mind when I give you these partial phrases: "Only the good die . . . [young]" or "A picture is worth . . . [a thousand words]" or "Blondes have more . . . [fun]." These words come as a package in our history. If the words are painful (try this one: "I pretend to be a good person but deep down I'm _____"), we might try to erase them, but all we are doing is adding to them. Try it with any of these statements and you will notice that another word appears and you are initially pleased because it is not ____ [put in the forbidden word], until you realize that "___ is not ___" is yet another relation. There is no healthy eraser. This can be exactly like what is going on with clients. It can help to see how this game is impossible to win:

Therapist: Tell me, as a child did you believe in Santa Claus?

Client: Sure. We put cookies out and everything, I'd write a wish list.

Therapist: Do you still believe in Santa Claus?

Client: Of course not, but it's fun for the kids.

Therapist: Yeah. And when you see a rainbow reaching the ground, what's over there?

Client: [chuckles] A pot of gold.

Therapist: Funny, everyone says that. Not a pile of gold, not a pot of silver, but a pot of gold. Ever gone digging for it?

Client: [laughs] No.

Therapist: Back to Christmas for a moment. When you walk through the toy store in mid-December, what do you see?

Client: Santa, all the Christmas stuff, elves, reindeer.

Therapist: And what does that make you think of?

Client: Santa's toy factory at the North Pole.

Therapist: Now you don't believe in this stuff, right? But it still comes up. And when you see a rainbow, what pops up in your mind?

Client: A pot of gold.

Therapist: Where did these thoughts come from?

Client: I suppose we're told this stuff when we are kids, by our parents, other people.

Therapist: And this idea, you haven't done well enough in your life, that you've failed as a person. Where did that come from?

Client: I don't know, same place, I guess, stuff I've heard, stuff I've put together over the years.

Therapist: Yeah. And tell me, how would we get rid of the thought of a pot of gold, or the elves?

Client: Don't know, I guess we don't.

Therapist: So what about this other stuff—I've failed. . . . I'm not good enough, nothing I do is ever quite good enough, and all the dozens of variations?

A classic ACT technique is the What Are the Numbers? exercise we described in the previous chapter in the case of Sarah. If clients get a sense of the point, the exercise itself can be used as a form of communication: Why should we take our own thoughts so seriously, when they may be nothing more than conditioned events? How silly is it that we are at the whim of their showing up at any time? The point is not to convince clients that their thoughts are wrong, or useless, or silly, but to offer a context in which they can notice that thoughts can be automatic. Maybe your client needn't give such importance to those thoughts or engage in a struggle to change or get rid of them but, rather, can make room for them and let them be, while choosing to live his or her life.

This was done later in the work with Sarah, when discussing her anger and frustration with her mother (it is also worth noting that she is now spontaneously using more defused language as the result of the previous defusion interventions):

Therapist: It's something almost like "I'm bad for feeling that."

Sarah: Yeah. That's it. I think that's the bottom line. I mean all the other sentences come but the bottom-line sentence is "and that means, I'm bad."

Therapist: OK, [offering a tissue] so here comes "I'm bad." What are the numbers?

Sarah: 1, 2, 3.

Therapist: And if I get angry I'm . . .?

Sarah: Bad.

Therapist: OK, here we go. We'll just let that be there like that [laying the tissue on her knee]. Is that your enemy? Does that have to change before you can be there with yourself and allow yourself to feel what you feel even when your mind says you can't? It's just your conditioning. What are the numbers?

Reasons and Rules

Imagine you are 6 years old and you just punched your 4-year-old brother in the face. He is crying, and your parents are upset. They demand an explanation for this inexcusable behavior. What's wrong with you, why did you do it? As a scientific matter, you do not know why you did it: He did something, you felt something, you did something. Your parents are upset and start supplying you with explanations. "Were you angry?" they ask. "I guess so," you answer.

We learn at an early age to give reasons for our behavior. It makes sense from a societal standpoint; we need to teach members of a society to recognize markers that predict bad behavior, like "I feel angry," and we try to teach the rules of prosocial behavior ("No hitting or kicking. Nothing that hurts."). It is necessary, but there is an unseen cost. We begin to relate to our own behavior inside the context of reason giving. We begin to believe our own reasons. By the time we are adults, we are so trained in giving reasons that we can do it endlessly and with the sense that all of these reasons are True with a capital T. Inside that story, the results cannot change unless the reasons change—but often the reasons are beyond our control.

Clients present with well-rehearsed stories about why they are the way they are, why they do what they do, why they cannot change this or that behavior, or why they need to change how they think or feel before anything else can happen. Most of us have probably been alive close to a billion seconds, possibly more, some of us double that. We do not have conscious access to all of our experiences—only a very, very small subset that are either recent or have some kind of significance. Yet somehow we are sure that we know the causes of our behavior. It is silly, if you think about it.

The question for ACT is not whether reasons are True but whether treating those reasons as True is helpful. As with everything else in ACT, it is an issue of workability. Undermining the context of reason giving can create room for more flexible behavior. More flexibility means clients can look at reason giving as a process, something the mind does, and maybe in looking at that process can see that there is room to choose behavior, with or without a set of reasons.

A simple exercise, which can be helpful in all areas of defusion, is to have clients label their thoughts as thought.

Therapist: So you are saying, despite the fact that you really value intimacy, you just can't get out there and date.

Client: Absolutely not. I'm just too depressed right now, too sad, nobody would want to spend time with me anyway.

Therapist: And as you say that I can almost feel your mind interjecting itself into this conversation. Can you sense that? Like all of the sudden we're getting bombarded with thoughts?

Client: Yeah, that kind of just happens.

Therapist: What if we tried to get a little breathing room. From now on, when you say a thought you are having, start it off by saying, "I am having the thought that . . ." and then say the thought. So I'm too depressed to date would be . . .

Client: Um, I'm having the thought I'm too depressed to date.

Therapist: Exactly. How does that feel in relation to the first time you said it?

Client: Different, a little strange. Not as set in stone I guess.

Right Versus Wrong

Have you ever felt that you had been wronged in some way, that you had parents who were unsupportive, or an unfaithful partner, or a friend who betrayed you, or a boss or colleague who treated you unfairly? Or maybe you were exposed to harassment or trauma. Past hurts can linger in the form of memories, unpleasant feelings, and intrusive thoughts. At some point in your life, you may have had the thought that this past hurt is ruining your life, that it is another person's fault that this happened, and that if this wrong could be righted in some way, or if it had just not happened, then everything would be OK and you could move on and live your life.

That situation is like one in which two crap tables are set side by side, and you can choose to play on one or play on the other. If you're going to play on the first one, you can play for being right. But here's the problem: The little chips you have to pay to play are slices of your own vitality. Conversely, over at the second table, you can play for vitality, but the chips you're going to need to play are slices of your own self-righteousness. So which game do you choose?

The problem with being right as a goal is that it creates behavioral rigidity. That is especially true with the kinds of issues clients face:

Therapist: So, if your father hadn't been so critical of you when you were growing up then you wouldn't be so anxious now?

Client: Well, yeah, he yelled at me so much, and seemingly for no reason, that I just never feel comfortable, and I'm always worried about when the next bad thing is going to happen to me.

Therapist: No kid deserves to be treated that way. And yet I'm also wondering if there is a part of you that is really invested in keeping Dad on the hook. What if you could rapidly move ahead now, without any change in your history? You have closer friendships. You pursued and obtained a fulfilling job. What would you imagine your dad would feel looking at that?

Client: He'd feel vindicated. Like he was some great parent.

Therapist: And what would that feel like?

Client: It wouldn't feel that great, because, I mean, he was awful to me, and it would be like giving him a free pass on all that stuff.

Therapist: So it's kind of like this, what happened to you when you were younger was a crime, so to speak. I even agree with that—it wasn't fair. But now your mind wants to make sure your life is the evidence that a crime was committed. Your life becomes the dead body that proved that a murder took place. So if you move ahead powerfully from here, you are going to have to be willing to carry some thoughts with you, like "'He's getting a free pass" and "This isn't fair." But whose life is this? It is yours or it is your painful history's?

This message can be especially painful when past hurts are extreme, for example, in cases of trauma or marginalization. It requires compassion and deep appreciation for how painful it can be. It is important for you, as a therapist, to have worked through your own issues when you use these methods, so that letting go of right versus wrong in order to move forward does not come off as invalidating.

That caution is true of all defusion methods. The place from which you can be effective and compassionate in doing defusion is one in which you know how hard it is to let go and step back from the usual way of relating to our thoughts, not knowing what will happen when you do that.

Acceptance and Willingness

We all struggle with having unwanted feelings, such as sadness, anxiety, shame, and anger, or with the absence of desirable feelings, such as happiness, love, excitement, or contentment. Think of that feeling that you get when things are not going well in your life, when it just seems like the cards are stacked against you, or that people are not on your side, or that you just are not good enough. Give it a name. Now try to remember the first time you might have felt that feeling. Think way back, as far as you can go. Was it yesterday? A week ago? A year ago? More?

For most, that feeling probably goes back a very long time, perhaps to when you were a child. Unwanted feelings have often been around since we began to remember, and a struggle to *not* have those feelings has been going on for just about as long. ACT teaches acceptance as a healthy alternative to running away from feelings. Clients are often confused by the word *acceptance* because they may have their own connotation for the term—usually, some version of "I have to put up with the fact that this sucks and can't change." Therefore, it can sometimes be useful to talk about what acceptance is *not* before talking about what it is. Acceptance is *not* forcing yourself through, white-knuckling your life, wanting discomfort, liking pain, being a "big boy," snapping out of it, evaluating pain as good, tolerating pain, or resigning yourself to the fact that nothing will ever change. These are almost 180 degrees from what acceptance means in ACT.

Acceptance is the adoption of an intentionally open, receptive, flexible, and nonjudgmental posture with respect to moment-to-moment experience. The root etymology of the word *acceptance* is to receive what is offered. Think of acceptance as receiving the moment as one would a gift from a friend. Carrying a posture of acceptance forward into life requires behavioral willingness as well. You can think of willingness as a voluntary and values-based choice to enable or sustain contact with private experiences or events that produce them. In common usage in ACT, *acceptance* and *willingness* are often used virtually as synonyms; when used that way, they cover both the psychological posture and the behavioral actions that the two terms separately emphasize when defined more narrowly.

It can help to speak metaphorically to help a client get a feel for acceptance and willingness. Acceptance is carrying your pain with you as you would a picture in your pocket, honoring your discomfort the way you would honor a relative by listening closely, holding what your history is giving you the way a glass holds water, abandoning the battle with your pain the way a soldier would lay down his weapons to walk home. It is inherently a gentle, loving posture. It is emotional, aware, and present.

Acceptance has an all-or-nothing quality to it. It is a bit like jumping. You cannot partially jump, you can either jump or not jump. You can take a small jump or a big one, but in doing so you are giving up a bit of control. You are putting yourself into space and letting gravity decide when you hit the ground. It is inherently a bold move.

Often clients have failed to see the possibility of acceptance and willingness. It is just invisible. The two-switches metaphor can help describe that situation:

> Imagine you are looking at two switches on the wall. One of them is a sliding switch that reflects your level of anxiety. That is the one you've been focusing on. You've been trying to get that slider down so that your anxiety can get closer to zero, in order to live the life you want. And even being here with me is another attempt to set that switch to low. But I want you to notice there is a second switch next to it. It's a toggle switch, like the old light switches, and it turns willingness on or off. So you have two switches in front of you: anxiety is high, medium, or low; willingness is on or willingness is off. You've been focused on the anxiety slider—but doesn't your experience tell you that you don't get to set that one? What about that willingness switch? You set that one, no? So which would you rather work on— the one you can set or the one you can't? But, fair warning: If you switch this willingness on, I'll tell you what is going to happen to the anxiety slider . . . it's going to go down . . . or it won't. You can hold me to that absolute promise, I guarantee it!

Usually clients chuckle a little bit, but that is really the promise. The point is to let go of outcomes and abandon conditionality applied to your experience.

Acceptance is not hard in the sense of effort—but it is tricky. Place a book on your client's lap, then remove it:

Therapist: How much effort did that take to feel that?

Client: None at all, actually.

Therapist: OK, I'm going to put the book on your lap again, and whatever you do, try not to feel it. Don't notice it. Don't feel it. Push away all sensation all awareness. Completely. Try. How much effort did that take?

Client: A lot. And it's impossible not to feel it.

Therapist: And when you try to not feel other things in your life, isn't that the same thing? How much effort does *that* take? And what are you not doing in your life as you try not to feel what you already felt anyway?

The goal of acceptance is repertoire expansion. Acceptance work is in essence a kind of exposure therapy, but the goal is not emotion reduction. That may happen, but the goal is a broader, more flexible, and more voluntary repertoire in the presence of a previously repertoire-narrowing event. This can easily be done in the context of traditional exposure work after getting a willingness commitment from your client. So you might say to an agoraphobic, "OK, we're going to go to the mall and we're going to sort of feel what it feels like to be there," and the client says, "I'll try." Usually that means "I'll do it if it doesn't get too bad," but that's not willingness at all. There is no leap. Exposure can safely be limited only by time and situation, not by quality. If you can get a 100% willingness commitment, you can work a bit on response flexibility in the presence of unwanted thoughts and emotions. For example, you can ask the client to stand there with you and feel what her body feels like and to notice what thoughts are doing. If you sense that the person has moments of greater presence (metaphorically, like "dropping the rope"), you can add deliberate repertoire expansion—buy something, or find the person in the room that has the funniest hairdo, or notice which storefront here is most attractively done. This is not distraction, because you are not trying to help her get away from fear. This is amplifying the repertoire: It's attraction, not distraction.

Another move would be to find out what would be the most horrible thing that could happen to your client. Let's say it is fainting and losing control. You might say, "We can do it together. Why don't we just lie on the floor here together and roll around a bit and say 'Help, help!' and lose control?" It is challenging, but we have done things like walking into a clothing store and ordering a hamburger (for clients who are afraid of making fools of themselves) or lying on the ground and rolling around, saying nonsense words interspersed with "I'm out of control" (for clients who are afraid of losing control). Bold moves like this always require full permission, and it's best to be there doing them with your client. If you are not willing to make a fool of yourself, it is unreasonable to ask your clients to do so.

In session, acceptance work can set the stage for client willingness commitments out of session, and it can take a variety of forms. Again, the goal is to get your client to be willing to experience difficult emotions for a period of time, without conditions on how that experience happens, and also to encourage response variety in the presence of that emotion in an attempt to create behavioral flexibility. The Physicalizing exercise we mentioned with the case of George in Chapter 1 is an example. Another related exercise involves pulling apart and parsing out different aspects of overwhelming emotions: the Paper Clip Monster exercise. Overwhelming feelings are like huge monsters made out of paper clips. They look big and scary, and the total effect can be overwhelming, but if we stop to examine their individual elements, we find nothing really fearsome there. In this eyes-closed exercise, we ask clients to get in touch with the difficult feeling and then notice carefully what their bodies do. The goal is to drop any struggle and just notice each specific bodily reaction. So, for example, as each aspect is named, the therapist takes the client into that sensation in great detail—where is it located, where does it begin and end? As they are seen, the theme keeps coming back to "dropping the rope" with just this one thing, and then later just this one other thing. The focus then shifts to other dimensions of experience in the same way: emotions, thoughts, urges and behavioral predispositions, and memories. By breaking the seemingly unacceptable overall experience down into tiny elements and making room for each, eventually the paper clip monster itself is something that can be experienced as it is.

Another approach is to help the person see the cost of avoidance and its paradoxical role in increasing pain. One way to illustrate this is by using the Pain Versus Suffering Circles exercise. Draw a small circle in the middle of a sheet of paper and fill it with words representing the clean pain that comes from the gap between what the person wanted and what history and circumstance provided. For example, the person might have wanted a happy childhood, but Mother died and Dad was judgmental. Put "sad childhood" in the center. Add other early events like that—events that were painful regardless of how the person reacted to them. Now start writing just outside of that circle all the things the person did to deal with the pain in the inner circle. Usually that list will include many things done to push the pain away. It might have included numbing out, withdrawing, cutting, drinking, procrastinating, and so on. After adding several, draw a larger circle around them all, and ask if the pain was growing or shrinking. Almost universally the pain has grown. Write the words "more pain" just outside that second circle in a few places and then encircle it as well. You can do a couple more rounds of this if you wish—pain leading to reactions that in turn lead to more pain.

From an ACT perspective, you cannot do anything about clean pain. (Indeed, often you would not want to: Would Sam really want to erase the pain of watching his mother die?) But you can stop the circle from growing. That added pain is dirty pain—suffering that is created by needless attempts to control what is. Then what is left is the natural pain that comes from being a human being, being finite, and living a life.

Acceptance has a kind of vitality, a presence, a wholeness. You can feel it in your therapy sessions. You can see it in your client. But when you talk *about* it with clients, you almost always are going to go sideways. In fact, if we hear a therapist in supervision say, "We talked about acceptance," almost always we know there is a problem, because "talking about" is a matter of intellectual understanding, and most of what you need to do is create a context in which your client is willing to walk into pain, fully and without needless defense. That is an experience, not talking about an experience.

Another common pitfall occurs when a client comes back after having made progress. As life begins to open up a bit, the mind tries to reassert control. For example, clients will note with pleasure how ACT methods worked—but "worked" is as measured against the "feel very good" metric that caused the problem to begin with. Therapists who are not careful will fall into the trap. If a client comes in saying, "I think I'm making progress, thanks to therapy. I felt really great last week!" the therapist should try to refocus the client on what he or she *did* (e.g., taking a more open stance, engaging in values-based actions), not on the waxing and waning of emotions. In fact, an ACT therapist might say something like, "I'm sorry to hear that," which might confuse the client but can open a discussion about how attachment to having "good" feelings as an outcome can be just a detrimental as (and is functionally similar to) trying to avoid the "bad" ones. Success in ACT therapy is moving forward with values-based behavior in the face of barriers or challenges.

It can be frustrating to see this process because, from the outside, it is often obvious that the client will move ahead if he is willing, yet he keeps getting drawn back into struggle and avoidance. It helps to remember that willingness is between the person and the person in the mirror. It is not your job as a therapist to make a client willing. It is your job to point to the client's experience, including the cost of not being willing and his yearning for a more values-based life. Willingness is a choice somebody has to make on his own.

This is why reassurance often does not work. If you begin to promise and reassure the client, "Gee. If you're willing then you know something great is going to happen," you're basically saying this:

> Because I'm strong and I know and you presumably are not, I'm going to give you my strength by convincing you what your experience can't yet convince you of, which is, namely, if you do this, grand things will happen; trust me; it will work out.

The "I'm-strong-and-you're-weak" move can easily weaken clients. Instead, we assume the client is strong enough to stand with his or her own pain, given the right context of compassionate awareness. Life is asking each of us if it is OK to be in the present, experiencing the echoes of the past and intentionally creating a future. You cannot answer yes *for* your client; you can only empower the client's ability to do so.

Mindfulness

Imagine a typical day. You get up, go through your morning routine, maybe eat, maybe have some coffee, take a shower. Maybe you linger, or maybe you are chronically late and are rushing around. What are you doing? What are you aware of? Imagine your drive to school or work, or walk, or train ride, or bus ride. What is going on? What are you thinking about? What do you notice? And now think of your day. What do you do? Whom do you interact with? What kinds of things are happening inside you?

For most of us, we go through the motions, on automatic pilot. It is human nature. We adapt to our circumstances, become efficient. We do what we need to do with little awareness of what is going on around us or what is going on inside us, unless something unusual happens.

As we sleepwalk through our days, we miss life happening all around us. You have seen the bushes and trees outside your house countless times, but when was the last time you really noticed them? Noticed the color shades, the grains, how the leaves gently blow in the wind? When was the last time you *experienced* them? And the sky, a different shade every day, with different clouds. And the sounds, always changing. Even if you think you've heard them before, you are always hearing sounds for the first time.

ACT teaches *mindfulness,* or present moment nonjudgmental awareness, as an alternative to our dominant mode of being. Mindfulness is certainly not something new to ACT, having been around for thousands of years in the mystical wings of religious traditions (not only Buddhism but all other major religious traditions as well). Mindfulness is an emphasis of psychotherapeutic approaches such as mindfulness-based stress reduction and dialectical behavior therapy, among others. However, it is also an essential component of ACT, particularly when considered in the context of how it relates to other ACT processes.

To do acceptance and defusion work, you must first have the ability to at least notice and label what is going on inside you. How can you be aware that your drinking functions to numb your feelings of sadness if you cannot become aware of feeling sad? How can you defuse from the thought "I'm a failure" if you cannot notice you are having a thought at all? And how can you orient to values as a guide for behavior if you cannot get grounded in what is happening right now and what is important to you in this very moment of life? Indeed, a certain degree of mindfulness skill is foundational for ACT.

Your clients' ability to tune into what is going on inside of them will vary. As an ACT therapist, you will want to assess this early and provide experiential work that will help your client be more effective at tuning the awareness dial. A common mistake of beginning therapists is to simply have clients try to do longer, classic ACT closed-eyes exercises only to find out that their clients fell asleep or lost focus after a few seconds. Instead, you want to introduce the concept of mindfulness early and revisit it frequently throughout therapy.

It may be helpful to start with very basic, in-session mindfulness exercises, usually conducted for about 5 minutes, such as focusing on breathing, noticing sounds, and scanning the body for different sensations. It is also common to assign mindfulness homework to ACT clients between sessions, especially early in therapy. Make sure to check in with your client after each and every exercise to see if he or she was able to participate and tailor your exercises to the client's skill level.

> Noticing the Breath: I'd like you to get into a comfortable position, feet on the floor, eyes closed, and simply follow the sound of my voice. Start by taking a few deep breaths. As you do, see if you can focus your attention on your breath. You may do this by focusing on the point at which the air enters and leaves your nose, or perhaps by noticing the rise and fall of your chest. Simply focus your attention on your breath for the next couple of minutes. If you find your attention wondering to thoughts, or feelings, or other sensations, that's perfectly OK, gently bring your attention back to your breath.

You may find it useful to start each session with a brief mindfulness exercise (2–3 minutes) to get the client (and yourself) centered in the room. A simple version of this would be to just say, "Before we go on, just notice what it feels like to be in this chair you're sitting in; I'm going to do the same with you. See if you can kind of notice where a chair begins and ends." You don't have to explain it. Just say, "Before we start this session, I just want to make sure we're in the room. So why don't you just close your eyes. Get comfortable. Get your feet on the floor. It will only take a minute or two." If people are afraid of closing their eyes, just tell them to put their hand over their eyes. Then just guide them into taking a breath, noticing the air coming in and going out, noticing the sounds in the room, noticing their heart beating, noticing where they touch the floor, and feeling what their skin feels like, or feeling the air movement. And then just ask them to picture the room when they take their hand off or they open their eyes and just come back.

Those 2 or 3 minutes will make you more efficient in the 50 minutes you spend with the client. The chatter will be less. There will be less of the initial dancing and telling stories about the last week that are not very useful. The client will be more present with you simply by being grounded in the moment. This can help the client (and perhaps you, too) to focus more broadly and clearly on the therapeutic agenda and the goals of the work.

Mindful walks can be useful as an intermediate step. You can do these with your client. You can pick something to focus on while walking around, such as the sights, and then switch during the exercise to, for example, sounds, and then finally orient to thoughts and feelings. In one mindful walk you can work not only on focusing attention but also on shifting that focus in a flexible way. Flexible application of mindfulness skills is the desired goal in ACT. With flexibility comes the ability to identify patterns of avoidance and notice alternative behavioral choices.

A closed-eyes version of this exercise is Sorting Into Boxes. Simply conduct an initial breathing mindfulness exercise (see the preceding example), and then ask the client to notice any thoughts, feelings, and bodily sensations as they show up, without trying to change or hold onto them. The client sorts each experience into one of three boxes: thoughts, feelings, or bodily sensations.

Start small and work up to more advanced skills. Give homework where necessary. Check in with your client often, to make sure he or she is able to follow what you are doing. You may find during therapy that it is useful to go back to basics, simply helping the client notice and label different experiences. Mindfulness homework can speed progress. Audio recordings, made by you or downloaded from the Internet, make structuring home practice relatively easy.

Perspective-Taking Sense of Self

Connecting with a sense of self that is transcendent and interconnected with others provides another dimension to life. It is a sense of self that is not threatened by what happens and by what changes.

We are speaking of "you" as the arena in which your experiences unfold. It contains thoughts and feelings, but it is not experienced as your thoughts and feelings. It contains your awareness of your body, but it is not experienced as your body. It contains your roles, but it is not experienced as your roles. It is something greater.

This continuity can be a powerful place in which to confront difficulties. A classic exercise is the Observer Exercise.

[Get the client to close his or her eyes, get centered in the room, and so on] I want you to remember something that happened last summer. Raise your finger when you have an image in mind. Good. Now just look around. Remember all the things that were happening then. Remember the sights . . . the sounds . . . your feelings . . . and as you do that, see if you can notice that you were there then, noticing what you were noticing. See if you can catch the person behind your eyes who saw, and heard, and felt. You were there then, and you are here now. The person aware of what you are aware of is here now and was there then. See if you can notice the essential continuity— in some deep sense, you have been you your whole life. Now I want you to remember something that happened when you were a teenager. Raise your finger when you have an image in mind. Good. Now just look around. Remember all the things that were happening then.

Remember the sights . . . the sounds . . . your feelings . . . . take your time. . . . and when you are clear about what was there, see if you just for a second catch that there was a person behind your eyes then who saw, and heard, and felt all of this. You were there then too, and see if it isn't true—there is an essential continuity between the person aware of what you are aware of now and the person who was aware of what you were aware of as a teenager in that specific situation. You have been *you* your whole life. Finally, remember something that happened when you were a fairly young child, say around age six or seven. Raise your finger when you have an image in mind. Good. Now just look around again. See what was happening. See the sights . . . hear the sounds . . . feel your feelings . . . and then catch the fact that you were there seeing, hearing, and feeling. Notice that you were there behind your eyes. You were there then, and you are here now. Check and see if in some deep sense the *you* that is here now was there then. The person aware of what you are aware of is here now and was there then. You have been *you* your whole life. Everywhere you've been, you've been there noticing. This is what I mean by the *observer you*. Notice how your body is constantly changing. Sometimes it is sick, sometimes it is well. It may be rested or tired. It may be strong or weak. You were once a tiny baby, but your body grew. Your cells have died, and literally almost every cell in your body was not there when you were a teenager, or even last summer. Your bodily sensations come and go. Even as we have spoken, they have changed. So if all this is changing and yet the you that you call *you* has been there your whole life, that must mean that while you have a body, you are not just your body . . . your roles . . . your emotions . . . your thoughts. These things are the content of your life, while you are the arena . . . the context . . . the space in which they unfold. As you see that, notice that the things you've been struggling with and trying to change are not you. No matter how this war goes, you will be there, unchanged. See if you can take advantage of this connection to let go just a little bit, secure in the knowledge that you have been you through it all and that you need not have such an investment in all this psychological content as a measure of your life. Just notice the experiences in all the domains that show up, and, as you do, notice that you are still here, being aware of what you are aware of.

In Chapter 3, we described how this sense of self emerged from verbal/cognitive relations that require perspective taking. That insight leads to many techniques that can be used to foster a more expansive and interconnected sense of consciousness. For example, a client might be asked to write himself a letter from a wiser future or to go back in time and meet himself when his problems first started and see if that person has compassion or wisdom to impart.

Values and Commitment

Close your eyes and imagine you are at your 85th birthday party. All the people you have touched in your life are magically there (even if they have died). One at a time, watch each person go up and speak on your behalf. Have each person say exactly what you would want her or him to have said about you, one by one. What did they all say?

The previous exercise is one used in ACT to uncover core values. Values are the guide by which therapy operates. Why should a client ask herself to open up to and fundamentally change the way she relates to thoughts and feelings, particularly deeply painful ones, unless it was in the service of something? ACT asks the question, "What do you truly and deeply care about, and are you ready to make your life about that and carry the rest along with you?"

Often clients put life on hold as they wait for their insides to line up. An obese person decides not to dance or go to the beach until he loses weight and feels better about his appearance. An anxious person decides not to pursue friendships until he can be completely comfortable socially. A betrayed lover decides not to date until she is not depressed anymore and feels "safe." In a sense, people try to win the war with their insides *before* they play the game of life. ACT challenges clients to start playing right now, identify what matters to them right now, and pursue what matters to them each and every day. A useful metaphor is building a house:

> Imagine that you decide to build a house by yourself. You draw the construction plan, you meticulously choose the materials, you carefully design the decoration. And meanwhile, you live with your

family in a little cabin across the street. And when the house seems finished and you could move in, you start thinking that maybe you could add a deck, so everything will be really perfect before you move in. Then, when the deck is finished, although your family can't wait to leave the little narrow cabin to live in the house, you start thinking that it would be better to install an alarm system before moving in. And so on. You delay the moving so as to make this house the most perfect of all possible houses, where your family will be perfectly happy and safe. And one day, you realize that the roof is beginning to show signs of wear. So you start working on repairing the roof. Then the plumbing gets old, and you have to redo everything from the beginning. And you still have not moved into the house. The house never stops being more perfect, and every day the moving is delayed. You spend more time preparing the life you wish to have in this house than actually living inside it. What kind of life do you want to live? Will you choose to stay in the cabin to prepare your future life in the house or to step in the house to fully live inside it now, to profit from its space and warmth in spite of its imperfections?

In ACT we talk about values as though they were a compass. We might explain that to a client like this:

> If you decide you want to move east, you can look at your compass and head in that direction. At the moment you do that, you are heading east. At no point do you actually arrive at east, but you can always check and reorient to the direction of east and keep moving.

We might even act this out with clients, taking a step in a direction, then another step. But we make sure the client understands:

> You may have destinations along the way (goals), but the destinations are not the direction. Value directions are important for figuring out, in any moment, what you want to be doing. If you do not know where you are going, you will not get there.
>
> An example would be, "What I want to be about is being a loving person." You would never clap your hands and say, "Well, OK. I finished that!" At the point in which you open up to actually caring

in that way and admitting to yourself that, for whatever reason, that's what you want to be about, you are already doing some of the actions of being about that, and every step along that path will continue such actions. It will never be finished. No matter how much loving you've done, there is more loving to do. This is very different from "I want to make a million dollars" or "I want to own a BMW." Money and cars are things that you can seek out, and when you get them, they are done.

However, people often confuse goals for values. Things like money and possessions often front as values, with the result that they can end up sort of hollowing a person out. You might find an excellent example of this in yourself or those around you. People with advanced degrees have done a lot of work to get that degree. The degree was a goal. The pursuit of a goal has a beginning and an end that can be fully achieved, and, yes, that end can be something that you want. It is part of a valued path, but getting it depends on a certain amount of activity. And once you get it, you've got it, it's done. A degree is like that, but if you ask the people holding the degree, "What is the value underneath that?" very often, there is a long pause. People can find themselves lost when they finally get that advanced degree, because they had a secret agenda, such as feeling more confident, or achieving some kind of status: "People will think highly of me," or "Then I'll feel important." Those are the folks who tend to have problems because they find out that they do not feel any smarter or more confident or important than they did the moment before they got the degree. Core values from an ACT perspective are not about feeling or thinking differently.

We are talking about chosen qualities of action that are present from the moment they are embraced and are never completely finished, being more like a direction than an object that one can obtain. When working with clients, we might say, "What I'm talking about is something that you really, really want to manifest." The choice of language offers one way of detecting value; the client is more likely to be talking about values in an ACT sense when using verbs and adverbs: to be a loving partner or to work well with others. If you are hearing nouns, you are probably dealing with goals, and the client is not there yet. There is a danger of becoming "mindy" and literal in this whole process—minds will try and say what they think values "should" be. There is a danger that people can take this vitalizing force, turn it into a stick, and beat themselves about their head and ears with it: "I'm not living my values, and I am an awful person because of it!" You have to guide clients toward what is meaningful to them, while making room for judgments in a defused way.

It is useful to establish nonjudgmental ground for the client's exploration of values:

> Suppose no one would ever know. It was just between you and the person in the mirror. What would you want to be about in this domain? Suppose no one would ever find out. There's not going to be any applause. Nobody else is going to weigh in on this. It's just between you and you. What do you really want in your life?

The therapist will have to filter out a lot of the superficial things and cut through plays at avoidance. And then the therapist can push them a little bit: "Is that what you really want, is that what you're playing for, what you really want your life to be about is that you don't feel fear, or that you're never sad?" At that point both client and therapist may realize that a goal like that is not about anything, really. It is just about comfort or relief of pain or whatever, which is a very limited agenda, one that got them into therapy in the first place. Again, if no one was going to laugh, and no one's going to giggle, and the client really could be about anything in this domain, what would he or she choose to be about?

An important aspect of values is that they are chosen. The issue of choice is a tricky one for most clients. One way to illustrate this is by simply picking two objects in your office and asking your client to choose one or the other.

Therapist: Which of these would you choose, if you're going to have one of them versus the other?

Client: [picks one]

Therapist: Why?

Client: I like it better [or it's pretty, this one tastes better than that, etc].

Therapist: Well, I didn't ask you which one you like better [or which one is prettier, tastes better]. I asked you to make the choice here and not your wants, desires, and likes to make the choice.

Client: I don't understand.

Therapist: Would it be possible to notice that that one's prettier, this one tastes better, and still have chosen the other one?

Client: I suppose, yes.

Therapist: It's a free country, right?

Note that you might have to repeat this a few times. Some clients might have a hard time breaking through that process and seeing that it is possible to say, "I choose that one." If they are struggling with it, you can make the choice even simpler, for example, by holding out your hand and saying, "Quick. Left or right?" What you are trying to get them to see is that it is possible simply to choose something and to let your mind chatter on about why but not actually link to it and defend it that way.

From an all-seeing, all-knowing place, there is a reason why animals choose left or right in an operant chamber or in a T-maze, for example. There is a reason in the sense of the history, but the animal does not know what that is, and the animal is not defending it. It is simply behaving. Humans climb inside the verbal regulatory organ we call the mind, fuse with it, and conclude that everything has to be explained, justified, and even determined by it. Why is that so important for values? Your mind is going to give you 101 reasons why you can't value something, or you must value something, or why you are never going to succeed with it, and so on. Furthermore, if you think it through logically, if values are like picking a ruler that you can then use to measure things (your actions), what is the ruler that would allow you to pick the right ruler? It is logically inconsistent. There cannot be right or wrong values because, by definition, your values are how you are evaluating your own behavior. Values are the ruler. They are, in a sense, preanalytic.

If everything must be perfectly verbally explained, justified, and reasoned, where does that ever end? It is like you are in a box, and you end up having to do what mama told you, what you think you are supposed to do, or what you are trying to do in order to manipulate your private events to avoid things, to not feel such guilt or pain or shame, etc. It can be a huge relief for clients, who sometimes have a sense of revelation, that it is possible, for example, for a person to pick 7UP over Coca-Cola simply because he picked it, and then watch his mind give him reasons. This is a place from which meaningful values work can be done.

Values are also process oriented. The value is in the doing, not in any particular outcome. One way to illustrate this concept is with the hiking metaphor:

> Suppose you enjoy hiking, and I ask you what the purpose of hiking is, and you say that it is to get to the top. Now imagine getting ready to hike, putting on your gear, packing your snacks, arranging to go with your partner or friends, and then arriving at the trail head. As soon as you get there, I show up in a helicopter, pick you up, take you to the top, and drop you off. Was that hiking? Of course not. Hiking is not arriving at the top, or finishing the loop, it is what happens in between.

One last distinction is that feelings are not good guides for behavior, and thus they are also not useful for values work. If you chose to be a loving partner but decide to be loving only when feelings of love for your partner were present, what would happen? You probably would be a pretty terrible partner. Part of being a partner is showing up when things are decidedly not pleasant, when feelings of love are difficult to come by. And thus, with values, it is important to separate them from feeling any certain way.

Values are sometimes hard to follow partly because they are linked to the pain we feel in our lives. By definition, if you care about something, you can be hurt by it. If you love your partner deeply, your partner can hurt you by cheating on you or not supporting you. Engaging the vitality of living requires that you open up to the possibility of pain. It is like two sides of the same coin. A place where you care deeply is also a place where you can be hurt. And usually, as you step toward things that are valued, painful things happen fairly quickly. And your logical mind says, "Going in that direction is going to be painful. I will protect you, and the way I'll protect you is by keeping you from doing that."

For example, if you dig down, 99% of people want to be about being connected with other people. They want to be in an intimate relationship because that's how humans are organized. But then if you ask people about their betrayals and the disappointments, if they have lived long enough on this planet, they know that sometimes it hurts to care about people because other people let them down, or other people actually betrayed them in important ways. And if you find that, you can ask, "Well, then, what were you tempted to do? What does your mind tell you to do?" And what our minds tell us to do are things like this: "What I'm going to do is never be that vulnerable again, never be that connected again, never that open again." Well, that's really, in a sense, creating the harm and multiplying it now to an even greater degree. Now something a person cares about deeply is off limits.

Acceptance and defusion are means of teaching people how to carry the pain that comes from the vulnerability and disappointments of caring. Values work is defining what a person really cares about. It is not a prediction. It is not an evaluation. We are not asking people, "Have you been a good boy?" We are not asking to predict whether or not the person would be able to do this. This is different. It is getting down to the gut: If you could be about anything, what would you be about?

There is an ACT saying: In your pain you find your values, and in your values you find your pain. You can see this process in the case of Sam, the young man dealing with his mother's death. After exploring painful memories, and appreciation, and loss, and other reactions, he naturally began to dig into the issue of values.

Sam: I've sort of put my life on hold. I'm going through the motions and just existing. I have a lot of passion in me, but I can't let it out. There are a lot of things I don't even do anymore.

Therapist: Give me an example, what is something you've given up?

Sam: I gave up playing guitar. I played classical and jazz guitar and I was very good. Very good. Then I just gave it up. I love music. I love what it says to me and to others. I love the creativity of it. But I never play anymore.

Therapist: If you were to play, what would show up? Take your time to imagine playing and see if you can sense what happens.

Sam: I just don't feel that passion for it. Plus my guitar teacher died much the same time that my mom did. Except way fast. I never even got to say goodbye. I trained with him for 9 years and then one day he was gone.

Therapist: Slow this down a little. It turns out there is pain even here in a place close to your heart. A place you can be creative; be yourself; create beauty. Am I putting words in your mouth?

Sam: No, it's exactly like that. [tearing up] It seems like I can't be myself anywhere.

Therapist: Slow down. This is worth your attention.

Sam: It's worse since my mom died. She used to sort of hide behind my door listening to me practice and play. And when I stopped suddenly there would be this clapping. I thought it was dumb at the time but really it's sweet. She just loved the music. Me, too.

Therapist: That sweet, yeah. Sam, you're a young person. You know, the things that we're trained to do with emotions by just growing up, and living in our culture, and by how our minds work are not necessarily the things that work with emotions. It's kind of hard to step up to some of the pain and your mind tries to protect you and it tells you what protects you is to not go there. Let's try to hold this the way you might hold something delicate. You say you don't have the passion for it, and yet I saw you tear up when you talked about the joy of playing and being yourself, creating. It wasn't just tears of sadness.

Sam: I love to play, to create. It sort of opens me up. But that scares me too. I have like this floodgate of emotions that if I open this it's going to overwhelm me.

Therapist: Well, it is true, that is, if you've spent a lot of time holding things away you have some work to do. That's true. But what I want to touch here is the possibility of something else. It is not just pain that life is asking you to open up to; it's purpose, meaning, vitality. It's living. If you open up to that, yes, the pain of losing your teacher will come back; yes, the pain of losing your mother will come back; but also music will come back; creating will come back; being yourself will come back; life will come back.

Sam: Funny thing. I get really angry about people who are fake and just about society telling us what we have to be.

Therapist: Yeah. I get that.

Sam: But yet I continue to pretend and I continue not to do things that make me who I am. I'm just hypocritical.

Therapist: Well, thank your mind for the tongue lashing. You know, minds are judgmental and they'll harass you about everything on every side, but it seems like you've touched something here that's important. This is not about wallowing around endlessly in grief. It's about giving you the space to be yourself. That is why avoidance is so toxic. It says you can't be yourself.

Sam: I see that. It's a package.

Therapist: Exactly. But this is cool. Really cool. We've touched something really basic. We've touched what you want. Like, here's the piano, if you go down and sit to play a piano what's going to come up? Loss. Pain. Memories. And music, creativity, and being yourself. Like, what if we could just let the mind do its thing and you do your thing. Whose life is this anyway?

Sam: I've been giving it away in pieces. It's like to numb out I have to die a little. It's not worth it.

If you can get a client to touch a core value and to give voice to it, you have changed therapy, because it is not easy to walk away from a core value once seen. And a lot of the dance you see around what is or is not important is because it is as though there is a secret. People learn to not even say out loud what they want, because other people can hurt them, because they can laugh at it, because even saying it makes them vulnerable.

Another pitfall is the *yes, but.* When you ask people what they want to be about, you may get something like this: "I want to have a good relationship, but my mother, she won't answer my phone calls." Hey, wait a minute. This is when you, as the therapist, chime in:

> This is not about her. This is about you. If you want to be about that, and then connect with that, then you behave how you want to behave. The rest is out of your control. There are lots of situations

where life does not give you the opportunity to actually manifest fully in the world of behavior in relation to a value. That does not mean that there is no value in connecting with what you care about. Regardless of outcome, following values can humanize and dignify what it is to live your life.

One worry of beginning therapists is that clients will choose things to value that will be hard to support. For example, clients might say, "I want more sex and money." People will do that, and so what you want to get into is what is inside being about "sex and money" and what it is like to be a person who is playing for that. It's often about feeling or not feeling a certain way, rejection, admiration, running from self-doubts or negative feelings. When you settle on something more core, you will likely see emotional reactions as someone owns up to what is so hard to say. You will see a sense of vitality. You will have a sense that a person is not so defended but is more open to different ways of going if it would lead in another direction. Mostly people will mention things like love, acceptance, contribution, participation, supporting others. You will see people in front of you who are very much like you, but they have been running from their own sense of caring in order not to hurt. You can tell them:

> You can be about what you want to be about now, and just like when you turn east, you are headed east from that moment. At the moment you turn and face your history, and all of your chattering mind trying to defend you from being you, and the vulnerabilities that come from caring and you admit that you care, you have created a whole different road map for therapy and for your life.

At this point you will want to get clients actively engaged in living. This is the commitment aspect of the ACT model. It is similar to behavioral activation but in the context of acceptance, mindfulness, and defusion and guided by deep values clarification. Virtually anything that helps get clients to engage in behaviors consistent with values can fit in this phase. Goal setting works. Making small commitments works. Noticing patterns of behavior that contribute to suffering, and deliberately stepping out of those patterns and doing something else, is important.

It takes courage to act in the service of values. It takes boldness. A therapist might ask:

> If you were to live boldly today, what would you do? If nothing were off limits, if you were not focused on whether or not an outcome would occur, or whether or not people might think differently about you, or whether or not it would feel good . . . what would you do?

As the therapist, you might spend portions of each session simply making behavioral commitments and then debriefing the barriers that rose up when your client tried to stick to those commitments.

ACT therapists often make commitments alongside their clients. We all could stand to live a bit more boldly. We all have some areas of our lives that are off-limits or could use the shine of a light now and then. And indeed, disclosing about areas you struggle with, standing alongside your client and saying, "This is hard for me . . . and I'm going to do it this week," can be a moving and humanizing therapeutic process. Once again, as with other aspects of ACT, your ability to connect with and embrace ACT processes will impact your ability to help your clients do the same.

Creating Overarching Metaphors

It helps to put the whole ACT process into exercises and metaphors that organize the work. That was done with Sam, following his realization that avoiding pain had led him to try to live in a way that was not true to himself.

Therapist: It's kind of like that game we played as children: Follow the Leader. Think of yourself as a leader in that game. You have a lot of things following you. Your sadness over your mother's death is following you. Your loss of your teacher is following you. Your judgment that you are a hypocrite is following you. If you're really determined not to have them talk or not to have them be in there, you have to spin around, stop going where you were going, and try to get them to leave or shut up.

Sam: That is really good. It is just like that.

Therapist: But part of what's important to you is not just being what society tells you to be, but being true to yourself.

Sam: Yeah. That is very important to me.

Therapist: And that is what a leader is. These followers are your memories, your pain, your thoughts. Nobody else's. This is not the culture. This is not society. This is yours. This is part of your life. Is it OK to be you with all of that stuff in line behind you?

Sam: So, are you maybe saying that I need to become comfortable with them being there?

Therapist: Here's the sense in which that's true. The word means to get with your strength. *Com* means "with"; *fort* is just like "build a fort," it means "strength." When you try to make the followers go away, or ignore them, or just pretend they're not there, or do what they say, do you get with your strength?

Sam: The opposite.

Therapist: And when you let them follow, when you learn what they have to teach you and still keep your eyes and heart on where you want to go, what does that feel like?

Sam: Strong.

Therapist: So I would say, yeah, get with your strength, but it's more like comfortable the *action* not comfortable the *emotion*. It's being with strength even with the leader that says, "Hey, I hate having all these followers!"

Sam: Yeah. Yeah. I think I know what you mean.

Therapist: It is like life is asking you a question: "Is it really OK to be you? Really?" Can you do what you deeply care about, even with your history as it is? If you can get to that place where it's like, "OK, followers! We are going marching!" then, you know, you've got a pretty powerful place you can live your life.

Sam: Well, that's what I'm going to do. I need to learn more about how, but that's what I'm going to do.

The Case of Sarah

Earlier in this chapter we promised to revisit Sarah and see where things went.

Therapist: OK. But there is an odd thought in here. Inside, "I'm not going toward anger because I shouldn't feel that", is it fair to say that you're doing to yourself the opposite of the kind of relationships you want from others? If it hurts not to be seen for the person that you are, when these emotions can't be seen, can't be made room for, aren't you sort of doing the same thing to yourself?

Sarah: Say that again. I didn't quite get it.

Therapist: What I'm asking you is, is it OK to be you, with your feelings and with your thoughts, as they are, not as you judge them to how they should be?

Sarah: Can I be OK with who I am and what I'm feeling? That is hard for me. I'm realizing it as I'm saying it. I'm always judging myself that I should be like this or I should be like that, which is kind of the same thing I said she did! [laughing]. Ah! I hate that about life!

Therapist: [laughing] Yeah. But you know if you go into pain, sometimes it teaches you things. What if this pain teaches you something about what you want? What you want from your mother but also what you want . . .

Sarah: For myself. Yes, for myself.

Therapist: So when people are interacting with you in a way that makes you feel as though you're invisible, that hurts. You feel angry about it. If we were to flip that over, what does it show about what you care about? Let me state it another way. What would you have to *not* care about for you to *not* be hurt when you're not seen?

Sarah: I care about being seen. I want to be genuine. I want to be real. I want to be known.

Therapist: Where have you been going instead?

Sarah: When I get angry then I go with the shoulds. You shouldn't be angry. Why are you doing that? That's not fair to her. But next thing you know I want to get off the phone.

At this point it is becoming clear that Sarah's relationship values are essentially the same as the psychological flexibility model. She wants relationships that are accepting, active, values based, aware, attentive, and nonjudgmental. But she is treating herself in exactly the opposite way. This sense of a values violation elevated the importance of acceptance, defusion, and mindful awareness, and therapeutic efforts focused on them took on new vitality. The case concluded on a positive note:

Therapist: What I'm suggesting is more like a path that might be there for you to follow by finding a way to be more accepting and mindful of your own processes. And to do with yourself what you say . . .

Sarah: I want from her.

Therapist: You want from her.

Sarah: Oh, be accepting of myself! OK, I get it. That *is* what I want from her. But I'm not doing it for myself. I need to get practice in doing it. Right now all I'm doing is running.

Therapist: Yeah, exactly. But I think even seeing that and seeing the cost is useful. It opens up an alternative.

Sarah: Yes, it does, and you really made me hopeful that there will be a path that I can get to. I've been praying to God. You've given me hope.

ACT AND CULTURAL COMPETENCE: USING PSYCHOLOGICAL FLEXIBILITY AS A TARGETED ANCHOR

There are data suggesting that modification of interventions on the basis of cultural knowledge can be practically helpful (Sue, Zane, Nagayama Hall, & Berger, 2009), but empirical progress in this area has been notably slow. One of the challenges is that cultural knowledge alone is not enough to ensure practical progress; cultures can and do promote processes that are psychologically unhealthy for their members. The cultural promotion of experiential avoidance (Hayes, Strosahl, & Wilson, 1999, 2011) provides a ready example. How then should ACT be modified for cultural competence?

The CBS development strategy underlying ACT (Hayes et al., in press; Vilardaga et al., 2009) suggests an approach: Link cultural knowledge to psychological flexibility processes. To the degree that these concepts are grounded in basic behavioral principles, they can provide a kind of targeted anchor for cultural modifications.

Consider the concept of reinforcement to understand what we mean by a *targeted anchor*. The principle of reinforcement is robust across cultures, but culture greatly modifies whatever functions as a reinforcer for an individual. Thus, at its best, knowing about reinforcement provides a target for studies of needed cultural modifications (because what functions as a reinforcer varies across cultural groups), but it also anchors cultural knowledge into a larger body of literature about learning processes (because reinforcement is a broad behavioral process).

In part because it is based on a contextual and learning approach, psychological flexibility processes provide good targets for cultural modification (Hayes, Muto, & Masuda, 2011). For example, values work in ACT needs to be fitted to different cultures by careful attention to the preferences of clients. Cues for avoidance differ across cultures on the basis of the social construction of emotion. Assessment of a perspective-taking sense of self in allocentric cultures might need to include collective deictic relations (e.g., we/they and not just I/you; see Nagayama-Hall, Hong, Zane, & Meyer, 2011). As Hayes, Strosahl, and Wilson (2011) pointed out,

> If cultural knowledge can be linked to principle-based processes, then cultural adaptations can be based on functional analyses rather than on the topographical features of cultural knowledge per se. There seems to be no reason why evidence-based cultural adaptation cannot be built into our models from the ground up. (p. 234)

The targeted-anchor approach to cultural modification needs to be examined in a step-by-step fashion; however, because the link between psychological flexibility and basic behavioral principles is still being researched, we cannot yet assume that, say, experiential avoidance is toxic across cultural groups. Psychological flexibility processes may not really turn out to be anchors in the same way as more basic concepts, such as reinforcement. To explore that issue, ACT researchers have begun studying the cross-cultural relevance of psychological flexibility. For example, because Asian cultures emphasize acceptance and mindfulness, we have examined whether psychological flexibility is predictive of psychological health with Asians in the same way as it is in other cultural groups. So far the data are very supportive (Cook & Hayes, 2010; Masuda, Wendell, Chou, & Feinstein, 2010).

CONCLUSION

The fundamental question that underlies the entire ACT model is the following: Given a distinction between you and the stuff you are struggling with (perspective-taking sense of self), are you willing to have that stuff fully and without defense (acceptance), as it is, not as what it says it is (defusion), and do what takes you in the direction (committed action) of your chosen values (values), at this time and in this situation (attention to the present moment)? For Sarah, the answer more frequently became yes as greater defusion and acceptance led to greater values clarity. We say "more frequently" because life may ask this question many times a day. As a therapist, your job is to get your client to see the choice and say yes more often. In the same way that you never "finish" valuing, psychological flexibility is never fully achieved or done. There will always be challenges and opportunities for growth.

5

Evaluation

A book of this kind is not the place for a comprehensive review of a rapidly growing research literature. Lists of empirical publications in acceptance and commitment therapy (ACT), relational frame theory (RFT), and psychological flexibility are maintained on the Association for Contextual Behavioral Science (ACBS) website (see References), and comprehensive reviews are now being written with some regularity about components of the contextual behavioral science research program, such as psychological flexibility (Chawla & Ostafin, 2007; Hayes, Luoma, Bond, Masuda, & Lillis, 2006; Kashdan & Rottenberg, 2010) and ACT outcomes (Hayes et al., 2006; Öst, 2008; Powers, Vörding, & Emmelkamp, 2009; Pull, 2009; Ruiz, 2010). Any review is quickly out of date because it is now uncommon for even a few weeks to go by without the appearance of important new evidence with relevance to some aspect of the program. Thus, our goal in this chapter is to reveal the general characteristics of the existing data. In broad strokes, what are the current strengths and weaknesses of the ACT evidence base?

To describe where we are without drowning in the details, we will make some statements without documentation. For example, if we mention that there are more than 50 randomized controlled trials (RCTs) on ACT, we will not then cite all of the studies. Between the ACBS website, the reviews just cited, and a good search engine, the statement can quickly be evaluated should the need arise. We will, however, give specific and cited examples in many areas so that the pattern of results in the current literature can be given some specificity.

DOES PSYCHOLOGICAL FLEXIBILITY HELP EXPLAIN PSYCHOPATHOLOGY?

The literature on psychological flexibility and experiential avoidance is large, and the results are consistent. Psychological flexibility and its various components negatively correlate with most forms of psychopathology (Chawla & Ostafin, 2007; Hayes et al., 2006; Kashdan & Rottenberg, 2010) generally in the $r = .35–.55$ range. This is not merely a correlational finding: Psychological flexibility predicts psychopathology longitudinally. For example, the psychological sequelae of exposure to traumatic events is predicted by baseline levels of psychological flexibility and experiential avoidance; Polusny et al. (2011) produced one of several such studies, even showing that parents' level of experiential avoidance predicts their children's longitudinal adjustment when exposed to trauma. Psychological flexibility also mediates other coping and adjustment strategies, such as suppression or cognitive appraisal, cross-sectionally and over time (Kashdan, Barrios, Forsyth, & Steger, 2006).

IS ACT AN EVIDENCE-BASED TREATMENT?

The standards for this question vary around the world, and individual researchers often have personal opinions about such things. However, in the United States, if the focus is on objective, peer review–based processes, the answer is yes. ACT is on the list of empirically based treatments maintained by Division 12 (Society of Clinical Psychology) of the American Psychological Association in the areas of depression and chronic pain and on the National Registry of Evidence-Based Programs and Practices maintained by the U.S. Substance Abuse and Mental Health Services Administration (SAMHSA) with studies cited in the areas of psychosis, worksite stress, and obsessive–compulsive disorder. The level of empirical support listed varies but is already strong in some areas. The number of areas in which ACT is viewed as evidence-based seems sure to rise because multiple controlled studies are now available in many other areas such as smoking and substance abuse, several areas of anxiety, and several areas of behavioral medicine. It should be noted that APA Division 12 and SAMHSA criteria have been criticized for a lack of emphasis on theory and process of change evidence (see David & Montgomery, 2011). A contextual behavioral science (CBS) approach embraces that concern, so inclusion on such lists is only one indicator of empirical support by the ACT community.

The meta-analyses of the ACT literature seem to agree that between-group effect sizes summarizing across all existing studies appear to be around .65, meaning that ACT showed between a medium and high effect when compared with a variety of control groups ranging from no treatment to current gold standard across a range of clinical presentations (more detailed comparisons to follow; Hayes et al., 2006; Öst, 2008; Powers et al., 2009; Pull, 2009; Ruiz, 2010). Follow-ups as long as a year and a half have not shown significant deterioration of effects (e.g., Westin et al., 2011), and indeed outcomes at follow-up have generally been slightly larger than outcomes at posttreatment (e.g., see Hayes, Wilson, et al., 2004).

IS ACT A TRANSDIAGNOSTIC TREATMENT?

The evidence suggests that the answer here is also yes. Perhaps the most dominant characteristic of the ACT empirical literature is its breadth. There are RCTs or controlled studies of other types (e.g., multiple baseline designs) in the following areas of mental health, among others: obsessive–compulsive disorder, generalized anxiety disorder, panic disorder, depression, polysubstance abuse, coping with psychosis, borderline personality disorder, trichotillomania, marijuana dependence, skin picking, and eating disorders.

There are such studies also in the following areas of behavioral medicine and physical health, among others: chronic pain, smoking, diabetes management, adjustment to cancer, epilepsy, whiplash-associated disorders, chronic pediatric pain, weight maintenance, exercise, work stress, and adjustment to tinnitus.

There are controlled studies of that kind also in many other areas of life: stigma toward substance users in recovery, racial prejudice, prejudice toward people with mental health problems, self-stigma in weight-maintenance, self-stigma in gay and lesbian populations, self-stigma among people in recovery from substance abuse, chess playing, promoting worker effectiveness, problematic pornography viewing, clinicians' adoption of evidence-based pharmacotherapy, and training clinicians in psychotherapy methods other than ACT.

As this book is being written, more than 50 RCTs have been published or are in press, and a new study of that kind appears once a month. When it is remembered that this work began in earnest in the year 2000, it is a surprisingly broad and lengthy list. These protocols are not all the same—often they differ in the behavioral methods they employ—but that in itself is part of the model. What is perhaps more surprising is how much these protocols overlap, given the breadth of the topics addressed.

IS ACT KNOWN TO BE MORE EFFECTIVE THAN OTHER EVIDENCE-BASED TREATMENTS?

Whether ACT exceeds other evidence-based treatments in effectiveness is arguable. Powers et al. (2009) reached the conclusion that the answer was no, at least not yet. In a reply to that article, however, we showed that their conclusion came from a handful of errors and several controversial decisions, such as categorizing carefully conducted evidence-based pharmacotherapy as treatment as usual instead of active treatment (Levin & Hayes, 2009). We agree that the literature is still quite young in this area, however, and more work needs to be done. At present, it would be safest to say that ACT works better than no treatment or treatment as usual and at least as well as other evidence-based practices when considered broadly.

IS ACT KNOWN TO BE MORE EFFECTIVE THAN OTHER FORMS OF COGNITIVE BEHAVIOR THERAPY?

ACT's effectiveness compared with other forms of cognitive behavior therapy (CBT)—a subset of the question just answered—varies; some studies show positive differences, and a smaller set shows negative ones. We are not yet ready to reach a conclusion, other than to say that it appears that, so far and in general, ACT is at least as effective as other forms of CBT when considered broadly; it may be more or less beneficial than traditional CBT when different subgroups of patients are examined; and, in most cases, it seems to work by characteristic processes of change rather than those drawn from other models.

ARE THERE EXAMPLES OF ACT FAILING TO DO AS WELL AS OTHER TREATMENTS?

Yes. For example, in a study of math anxiety Zettle (2003) found that systematic desensitization did a bit better than ACT on trait measures of anxiety (math anxiety outcomes were the same). A subsequent study with test anxiety (Brown et al., 2011) found that ACT and traditional CBT methods produced equivalent outcomes; however, in that study, when actual test performance and grades were examined, ACT did significantly better (objective performance was not assessed in the Zettle, 2003, study). A number of larger studies are coming, and a few reportedly have had negative results, so we will have to see. The number of studies with negative outcomes is still too small to detect a pattern, but there is some indication that ACT does better with more chronic, severe, or multiproblem cases. Learning how to apply it to lesser problems, prevention, and the like is a work in progress. It could be that the issues it raises (e.g., sense of self, role of emotions, life purpose) are just too fundamental for treatment of more minor problems, at least not without additional treatment development.

DOES ACT WORK ACCORDING TO ITS PUTATIVE PROCESSES?

The evidence is reasonably strong that the answer is yes, but more needs to be done. There are currently more than 30 mediational studies in the ACT literature. In almost all of them, post- or midtreatment measure of ACT processes (experiential avoidance, defusion, psychological flexibility, values) mediated differences between groups in follow-up outcomes, accounting for about half of the variance in outcomes (Hayes, Levin, Vilardaga, & Yadavaia, 2008). The reason we need to be tentative is that in most of these studies, outcomes had already changed when mediators were measured. This raises many methodological issues that need to be addressed very carefully. However, some ACT studies measured mediators before outcomes changed, and the findings seem to hold, suggesting that the mediational findings are likely not the artifacts of simultaneous measurement. What is most notable is the consistency of the finding, especially given the wide range of comparison conditions, the wide range of topic areas and outcome measures, and the small number of putative processes examined as mediators. It is also notable that when possible mediators are drawn from cognitive theory or other perspectives, they generally do not do as well in explaining ACT outcomes. An example is provided by a reanalysis of one of the earliest ACT studies (Zettle & Rains, 1989). In the original study, ACT was compared with cognitive therapy (CT) and with a modified form of CT that did not include distancing (on the grounds that if ACT was just distancing, this modified condition should do worse than the full package). In fact, the modified form of CT did better, but that confused the ACT-versus-CT comparison, so Zettle, Rains, and Hayes (2011) reanalyzed the difference between the two normal conditions (ACT and CT) using a modern intent-to-treat analysis (i.e., including all participants, even dropouts, in the analysis). ACT produced greater reductions in levels of self-reported depression. Posttreatment levels of cognitive defusion mediated this effect at follow-up, but the posttreatment levels of depressogenic thoughts or dysfunctional attitudes did not mediate outcomes, showing that putative processes underlying ACT did a better job of explaining outcomes.

ARE ACT COMPONENTS EFFECTIVE?

More than 40 studies of ACT components have been published; about a dozen are with applied populations seeking treatment, whereas the rest are with such things as laboratory-based pain tolerance or similar tasks and populations. At least some research has been done on all of the hexaflex processes. A meta-analysis (Levin, Hildebrandt, Lillis, & Hayes, 2012) found that ACT-relevant treatment components are helpful in isolation and combination, with significant positive effect sizes observed for acceptance, defusion, present moment, mixed mindfulness components, and values, plus mindfulness component interventions as compared with inactive intervention conditions. Larger effect sizes were found for theoretically specified outcomes, for differences between theoretically distinct interventions, and for interventions that included experiential methods (e.g., metaphors, exercises) rather than a rationale alone. Given the small number of studies done with actual clinical populations, however, this evidence needs to be viewed as supportive but not determinative.

ARE ACT PROCESSES EXPLAINED
BY RELATIONAL FRAME THEORY?

We think ACT processes are explained by RFT, but RFT is designed to explain human language and higher cognition, not just ACT. That said, research and development in ACT has been intertwined with that in RFT from the early days, as we discussed in Chapter 2. Development is neither bottom-up nor top-down—it is reticulated, with ACT insights helping to guide RFT and RFT insights helping to guide ACT. The ACT focus on the functional context rather than the relational context of cognition is a major insight of RFT. Conversely, RFT labs have successfully modeled how thought suppression tends to expand through cognitive networks (Hooper, Saunders, & McHugh, 2010), providing experimental evidence for its dangers as a coping strategy. Rapidly evolving RFT work on the deictic relations underlying a perspective-taking sense of self (e.g., McHugh, Barnes-Holmes, & Barnes-Holmes, 2004) is already leading to new assessment methods and to a notably greater emphasis in ACT on the interlink between acceptance and compassion. We expect this kind of reticulated interplay to continue to evolve.

ARE THERE DATA ON THE NEUROBIOLOGY OF ACT AND ITS UNDERLYING THEORY?

There are some data on the neurobiology of ACT, and more are coming. A review of some of the broadly relevant neurobiological evidence was provided by Fletcher, Schoendorf, and Hayes (2010). So far the data are quite supportive. For example, highly experientially avoidant participants tend to show more lateralization of brain activity when avoiding emotionally evocative events (Cochrane, Barnes-Holmes, Barnes-Holmes, Stewart, & Luciano, 2007), suggesting that experiential avoidance is governed by verbal rules, as the psychological flexibility model suggests.

CAN ACT BE HELPFUL TO DIVERSE POPULATIONS?

Racial and Ethnic Diversity

ACT methods have been studied around the world, not just in the United States and Europe. ACT is known to be helpful to East Asians in areas such as pain (Takahashi, Muto, Tada, & Sugiyama, 2002) and job performance (Kishita & Shimada, 2011). A recent randomized trial showed that ACT helped to prevent and ameliorate mental health distress in Japanese international students in the United States (Muto, Hayes, & Jeffcoat, 2011). A small RCT conducted in India showed that ACT helped with drug refractory epilepsy (Lundgren, Dahl, Yardi, & Melin, 2008); a similar study showed similar benefits for poor South African Blacks dealing with epilepsy (Lundgren, Dahl, Melin, & Kees, 2006). In the United States, studies with good representation from various minority groups, including Asians (e.g., Gregg, Callaghan, Hayes, & Glenn-Lawson, 2007; Masuda, Muto, Hayes, & Lillis, 2008; Muto et al., 2011) and African Americans (Gaudiano & Herbert, 2006), have shown good outcomes.

Age

ACT has been shown to be useful to children and adolescents (e.g., Wicksell, Melin, Lekander, & Olsson, 2009; Wicksell, Melin, & Olsson, 2007) and older people (Wetherell et al., 2011) as well as adults.

Cognitive Ability

ACT is useful to cognitively impaired populations of various kinds, including the chronically mentally ill (Bach & Hayes, 2002; Gaudiano & Herbert, 2006), developmentally disabled (Pankey, 2008), and clients with traumatic brain injury (Sylvester, 2011).

Alleviation of Prejudice, Stigma, and Self-Stigma

ACT has also been shown to be helpful in the alleviation of prejudice and its internalization by creating more psychological flexibility regarding prejudicial thoughts toward others and more focus on interpersonal values. ACT can reduce prejudice toward ethnic minorities (Lillis & Hayes, 2007), toward those in recovery from substance abuse (Hayes, Bissett, et al., 2004), and toward persons with mental health problems (Masuda, Hayes, et al., 2007).

ACT also alleviates self-stigma and shame in populations such as the obese (Lillis et al., 2009), persons in recovery from substance abuse (Luoma, Kohlenberg, Hayes, & Fletcher, in press), and gay and lesbian clients (Yadavaia & Hayes, in press).

SUMMARY

In a recent review of the development approach being pursued by the ACT community, Hayes, Levin, et al. (in press) concluded, "The contextual behavioral science approach seems coherent, reasonable, and distinctive, and it has now yielded a body of work that is substantial enough for it to deserve to be considered on its own terms." We have provided an overview of ACT-relevant data in areas of key importance to the approach. So far, the empirical evidence seems to be supportive of ACT and its development strategy.

6

Future Developments

Acceptance and commitment therapy (ACT) is not a technique. It is an overall approach to intervention, based on an applied and basic model, an approach to knowledge development, and a basic philosophy of science. ACT is a convenient name for attempts to develop and apply interventions within a psychological flexibility model.

The community developing ACT, the Association for Contextual Behavioral Science (ACBS), has been designed to scale psychological flexibility processes into the community itself. Open, nonhierarchical, and values based, the community has grown rapidly (as described in Chapter 2) by applying communitarian variants of psychological flexibility to ACT development itself. As a result, it seems likely that the future of ACT will be determined less by its originators and more by the community. Thus, although we discuss possible developments in this chapter, our focus is on what ACT processes and the ACT community suggests for possible future developments.

EMPOWERING INDIVIDUAL AND COMMUNITY CONTROL

At the end of ACT workshops, attendees often ask how they can become ACT therapists or when they should call themselves ACT therapists. The ACT community has a strange answer to that question that is in keeping with ACT itself. There seems to be agreement that therapists can freely call themselves ACT therapists when they are doing therapy to create more openness, awareness, and active engagement in their clients; when they are themselves open to new knowledge of how better to do that; when they are taking steps to remain aware of developments in how to do that; and when they are actively engaged in learning how better to do that. In other words, ACT therapists are defined by their interest in a path—by their intention and commitment itself.

Technological skill is encouraged by giving clinicians access to training and access to developmental tools. For example, books and videotapes target specific psychological flexibility processes in a process-by-process fashion for the sake of learning (e.g., Hayes, 2007; Luoma, Hayes, & Walser, 2007), and skills in these areas can be assessed with a widely used checklist of ACT competencies that can be found at the ACBS website (see ACBS, n.d.; also see Strosahl, Hayes, & Wilson, 2004). Methods of measuring adherence and competence are designed to be functional, not topography based, so that they can be used across many settings (see Plumb & Vilardaga, 2010), and efforts are under way to computerize adherence system training so that clinicians themselves can ensure that they are applying these discriminations as would experts. Learning tools such as these are constantly being developed by the community itself, and a large number of them are available for free on the ACBS website. The goal of all is to give practitioners the means to ensure skill development once they are committed to a learning path, rather than to create a hierarchy with developers on top declaring who is in and who is out.

This is a very different approach from the usual one in evidence-based methods, which is to certify therapists who successfully participate in training programs conducted or authorized by developers. This traditional hierarchical approach can work reasonably well if methods do not evolve or do not need to evolve. The problem with certification linked to hierarchy is that it ossifies the technology and tends to weaken the accountability of developers or early adopters. If *new* ideas and *new* developments occur, when should they be included in the list of what needs to be known—and who makes that decision? Typically the answer is that the developers make the decision, perhaps in conjunction with those already certified by the developers—but this creates a hierarchy that can easily become unhealthy. If the developer does not like or understand the new methods, they are unlikely to be added—even if they are very useful. This may explain why it has been difficult to abandon features of evidence-based treatments when component analyses lead to answers that do not fit putative models (e.g., see Longmore & Worrell, 2007). Conversely, when the developer has new ideas, these are often added quickly, with great fanfare, often long before clear empirical evidence that they add to the method's utility. The hierarchy grows, the money flows, and science becomes a cover for the whole process—but the system is not designed to foster rapid scientific progress under communitarian control, which is the goal of the different approach taken by the ACT community.

Recognized ACT trainers become so through a systematic peer review process—like applying for a grant—that is controlled by trainers themselves within ACBS. No money changes hands. It is emphasized that a person need not be recognized by ACBS to be an ACT trainer. When peers agree that the trainer is skillful, the trainer still will not be recognized unless he or she signs a values statement that was hammered out by the ACT training community as a whole. Trainers agree that they will not make proprietary claims for their training, will give away their protocols or make them available at low cost, and will not themselves develop certification programs for therapists.

One effect is that young people can enter into the development process quickly and begin to make a difference without having to check their own ideas or their healthy skepticism at the door. The future of ACT seems likely to show a further rise of a process of improvement that is values focused, open, communitarian, and nonhierarchical. The contextual behavioral science community is becoming the driving force in the development of ACT and relational frame theory (RFT). Its commitment is toward the central value of the organization, which goes far beyond ACT itself: promoting the development of a contextual psychology that is more adequate to the challenge of the human condition. That goal may never be reached, but the progress is found in the journey itself.

EXPANSION OF THE APPLICATION OF THE PSYCHOLOGICAL FLEXIBILITY MODEL

We can confidently predict that the psychological flexibility model will be applied even more broadly than it is now, going beyond the already wide array of problem areas that we described in Chapter 5. We expect to see more work in behavioral medicine and primary care, more work in business and industry, more work in problems of social concern such as racism or religious prejudice, and more work in education, prevention, and community development. Many of these areas already have one or two encouraging studies, so it seems highly likely that additional development is coming. Additional areas will emerge that are not yet on the radar screen.

TECHNOLOGICAL ASSIMILATION

Technologically speaking, ACT is rapidly being assimilated into other therapies, particularly within cognitive behavior therapy (CBT). So far this process has been most visible in the acceptance and defusion areas. Most new methods of CBT are now sensitive to the idea that the key to psychopathology is not the presence of difficult thoughts, feelings, sensations, and memories but the person's relationship to these events. Other aspects of psychological flexibility seem likely to begin to be given more attention. Many alternative models do not currently emphasize the importance of values, for example. If the psychological flexibility model is correct, failing to address values constitutes a deficit that needs to be corrected. If a treatment approach moves to add values work, a body of developmental work on values, already done by the ACT community, will be available. Other models properly emphasize contact with the present moment, but fewer have seen the relevance of deictic relations or of a transcendent perspective-taking sense of self. Again, these ideas seem likely to penetrate the mainstream. We expect that psychological flexibility will gradually come to be an accepted core of most contextual forms of CBT and perhaps some humanistic approaches as well.

In the history of psychology, assimilations of this kind have sometimes led to useless conversations based on the theme of "We developed that first." That could happen in the case of ACT, but it seems unlikely. For one thing, many of these methods and ideas are thousands of years old, but, for another, the ACT community has emphasized giving away knowledge rather than making proprietary claims, has focused on processes and procedures more than on manuals and syndromes, and has focused on community. It is in the interests of those whose lives we serve to have developments used; therefore, the development community needs to stay focused on putting new methods and refinements in the hands of those who need them rather than on who gets credit for methods that already exist.

DEVELOPMENT OF INDIRECT INTERVENTION METHODS

As we noted in Chapter 5, ACT can be moved into a wide variety of dissemination forms: individual sessions, groups, peer-based methods, books, computerized protocols, classes, cell phone applications, business-based sessions, and so on. These are some of the areas in which new methods seem especially likely. The use of indirect intervention methods is expected to continue to broaden and deepen because of the scalability of the model and the pragmatic commitments of the ACT community.

DEVELOPMENT OF PSYCHOLOGICAL FLEXIBILITY ASSESSMENT METHODS

Assessment in ACT initially was largely limited to traditional self-report and behavioral measures. These methods are now broadening, in part because of the underlying development model itself. We are beginning to see RFT-based assessment methods focused on psychological flexibility.

For example, new RFT-based measures of perspective taking are being used in psychological flexibility–based analyses of applied problems, such as social anhedonia (Vilardaga, Estévez, Levin, & Hayes, in press). Similarly, the RFT-based implicit relational assessment procedure, or IRAP (Barnes-Holmes, Murphy, Barnes-Holmes, & Stewart, 2010), is being used to measure a key part of the psychological flexibility model, openness toward emotions (Levin, Hayes, & Waltz, 2010).

VISIBILITY

Finally, it seems quite likely that contextual behavioral science itself will have increased visibility in psychology and in the culture at large. A journal entirely devoted to a contextual behavioral science approach (the *Journal of Contextual Behavioral Science*) will appear in 2012. There are clear indications that RFT is beginning to be noticed by mainstream cognitive science (e.g., see De Houwer, 2011). The proliferation of ACT books for the public is leading to a much greater visibility within the culture and the media. Within psychology, psychiatry, and social work, ACT is rapidly becoming more broadly known. Tens of thousands of clinicians have been trained in its methods.

What all of these trends seem to point to is that ACT and its underlying approach are now part of the landscape of ideas in behavioral science and the helping professions. All scientific theories are ultimately shown to be mistaken, given enough time—but it is not possible to find the limits of theories until their ideas are understood enough to be considered. As this very book suggests, that stage is being reached for ACT.

Summary

Acceptance and commitment therapy (ACT) is an intervention method that uses acceptance and mindfulness methods and commitment and behavior change methods to produce psychological flexibility. It is difficult to categorize using traditional divisions within clinical psychology. On the one hand, it emerged from a development and extension of behavior analysis, which gives it features commonly associated with fairly conservative forms of behavioral intervention (reliance on basic behavioral principles; functional analysis; opposition to cognitive causes and dualism). On the other hand, the specific areas of extension in cognitive science via relational frame theory (RFT) and its resulting concern over excessive rule-governed behavior have given it features that are commonly associated with the deeper clinical traditions and sometimes to less empirical wings of clinical psychology (embrace of issues such as spirituality, the therapeutic relationship, and mindfulness; experiential methods; the centrality of cognition and emotion; contextualistic assumptions that create similarities to constructivist perspectives). ACT is part of a larger knowledge development strategy called *contextual behavioral science,* which combines a communitarian approach and a reticulated scientific strategy focused on empirically supported processes and procedures.

Psychological flexibility is argued to be composed of six key processes, each of which can be inverted when needed to focus on key aspects of psychopathology: defusion/fusion; acceptance/experiential avoidance; flexible attention to the now/inflexible attention toward the past and future; a perspective taking sense of self/attachment to the conceptualized self; values/unclear, avoidant, or fused values; and committed action/inaction, impulsivity, or avoidant persistence. Thus, the model of psychological problems and the model of intervention are interlinked in a psychological flexibility perspective.

ACT developers and clinicians have developed a wide array of procedures to target these specific processes. Defusion methods quickly reduce attachment to thoughts by altering the social verbal context in which they occur through such methods as physicalizing their form or word repetition. Acceptance methods lead to exposure and active curiosity regarding emotions and other psychological reactions. Flexible attention to the now is encouraged through contemplative practice and other mindfulness methods. A transcendent sense of self is enhanced through manipulation of the deictic verbal relations that underlie perspective taking, such as I/you, here/there, and now/then. Values work is designed to promote a sense of choice over the meaning and purpose of behavior in a way that promotes vitality and intrinsic motivation. Committed action methods use behavioral change strategies to promote step-by-step skill acquisition and the construction of broad and effective behavioral patterns.

The therapeutic relationship is central in ACT, but it is itself interpreted from the point of view of psychological flexibility. ACT has been shown to work with a diverse group of clients: children, adolescents, and adults; highly able and cognitively impaired; rich and poor; majority and minority clients; Americans, Europeans, Asians, and Africans. The model is designed to be modifiable for cultural competence but in a way that is arguably more empirically progressive than current approaches, by linking cultural knowledge to psychological processes within the psychological flexibility model and to their roots in basic behavioral processes as amplified by RFT.

ACT and the psychological flexibility model have been evaluated in several dozen randomized controlled trials, a similar number of component studies, dozens of mediation analyses, and an expansive program of experimental psychopathology. Controlled studies have shown that ACT is useful in nearly every area of clinical psychology (anxiety, depression, substance abuse, psychosis, and so on), many areas of behavioral medicine (chronic pain, diabetes control, exercise, weight control, epilepsy, smoking cessation, tinnitus, and so on), and an unexpectedly large range of social problems (prejudice, ability to learn, workplace stress, and so on). ACT appears to work by modifying psychological flexibility and its elements, and its component processes are psychologically active. ACT has been acknowledged by various accrediting bodies around the world to be an evidence-based practice. In the United States, ACT is on the list of empirically based treatments maintained by Division 12 (Society of Clinical Psychology) of the American Psychological Association and by the National Registry of Evidence-Based Programs and Practices within the U.S. Substance Abuse and Mental Health Services Administration.

The future of ACT seems to include further assimilation of its methods and extension of its underlying transdiagnostic model into areas such as business and industry, prevention, social justice, and primary care. There will be greater use of indirect intervention methods, such as computers (e.g., the Internet, online instruction, e-mail), books (conventional and electronic), cell phones (social media), and tablets, in an effort to bring psychological flexibility out of the clinic and into the streets. Innovations in training and dissemination are on the horizon, such as the use of online training to use the model with greater fidelity. Larger funded studies are increasing in many areas. The contextual behavioral science development community, already thousands strong around the world, seems likely to increase in its size and impact.

The central aspiration of that community is the creation of a psychology that is better suited to the challenge of the human condition. By its nature that is an aspiration that will never be completely reached or totally fulfilled, but, by reaching high, the ACT community is making a difference in the prevention and alleviation of human suffering and the promotion of human health and development.

Glossary of Key Terms

ACCEPTANCE   Actively contacting psychological experiences directly, fully, and without needless defense, with curiosity, interest, and willingness to learn and without automatic rejection, behavioral domination, or attentional inflexibility.

ACCEPTANCE AND COMMITMENT THERAPY   A psychological intervention based on modern behavioral psychology, including relational frame theory, that applies mindfulness and acceptance processes, along with commitment and behavior change processes, to the creation of psychological flexibility.

ARBITRARILY APPLICABLE RELATIONAL RESPONDING   Learned relational responding that can come under the control of arbitrary contextual cues (those determined by social whim or convention) not solely the formal properties of related events nor direct experience with them.

BEHAVIOR ANALYSIS   A natural science of behavior that seeks the development of an organized system of empirically based concepts that allow the actions of whole organisms interacting in and with a context, considered both historically and situationally, to be predicted and influenced.

BEHAVIORAL PRINCIPLES   Ways of speaking about organism–environment interactions that are high in precision, scope, and depth and that help to predict and influence these interactions.

COGNITIVE DEFUSION   The reduction of the automatic domination of verbal/cognitive events by altering the linguistic context so as to increase ongoing awareness of thought and to reduce the automatic literal meaning of these events. The term is often shortened to *defusion,* but in all cases *cognitive* is at least implied.

COGNITIVE FUSION   The domination of verbal/cognitive events over other sources of behavioral regulation due to contexts that minimize awareness of language and cognition as an ongoing historical and sometime arbitrary activity. Sometimes shortened simply to *fusion,* it always applies to cognition or to the cognitive aspects of more complex events such as emotion.

COMBINATORIAL ENTAILMENT   A defining feature of relational frames that refers to the ability to combine mutually related events into a relational network under forms of contextual control that can include arbitrary contextual cues. Combinatorial entailment applies when, in a given context, A is related in a characteristic way to B, and A is related to C, and as a result a relation between B and C is now mutually entailed.

COMMITTED ACTION   A values-based action that is deliberately linked to creating a larger pattern of action that serves that value.

CONCEPTUALIZED SELF   Self as an object of verbal reflection, analysis, and evaluation.

CONTEXTUAL BEHAVIORAL SCIENCE   An approach to knowledge development within a natural science of behavior that emphasizes the creation of broadly applicable and accessible functional contextual models of human behavioral processes that are linked to behavioral principles.

CONTEXTUALISM   A pragmatic philosophy of science based on the root metaphor of an ongoing historical act in context as its analytical unit and utilizing a truth criterion of successful working as tied to a specific set of analytic goals.

DEICTIC FRAMES   Relational frames that must be acquired by demonstration relative to a particular perspective, usually that of the speaker. A simple example is *here/there*.

FUNCTIONAL CONTEXTUALISM   The underlying philosophy of science in ACT; a form of contextualism (see definition) with the analytic goal of the prediction and influence, with precision, scope, and depth, of whole organisms interacting in and with a context considered historically and situationally.

MINDFULNESS   A conscious contact with the present moment that is accepting, defused, and flexibly attentive.

MUTUAL ENTAILMENT   A defining feature of relational frames that refers to their fundamental bidirectionality under forms of contextual control that can include arbitrary contextual cues. Mutual entailment applies when, in a given context, A is related in a characteristic way to B, and as a result B is now related in another characteristic way to A.

PERSPECTIVE-TAKING SENSE OF SELF   A sense of self as a locus or perspective (the "fromness" of awareness) that is interconnected with the consciousness of others and at other times and places due to deictic relational frames.

PSYCHOLOGICAL FLEXIBILITY   The process of contacting the present moment fully as a conscious human being, as it is and not as what it says it is and, based on what the situation affords, persisting or changing behavior in the service of chosen values.

RELATIONAL FRAME THEORY   A theory that argues that the defining feature of language and higher cognition is the participation of these events in relational frames.

RELATIONAL FRAMES   Specific types of arbitrarily applicable relational responding that have the defining features of mutual entailment, combinatorial entailment, and the transformation of stimulus functions regulated in part by learned arbitrary contextual cues. Relational frames develop from a history of relational responding relevant to the contextual cues involved, rather than being based solely on direct nonrelational training with regard to the particular stimuli of interest or on nonarbitrary characteristics of either the stimuli or the relation between them. It is always an action and thus can be restated anytime in the form *framing events relationally.* Various families of relational frames have been identified.

RULE-GOVERNED BEHAVIOR   In its most general form, behavior controlled by a verbal antecedent, in the relational frame theory sense of *verbal* (see definition). In actual use, behavior that is controlled by verbal antecedents is more likely to be termed *rule governed* if the verbal antecedent constitutes a complete relational network that transforms the functions of the nonarbitrary environment.

SELF AS CONTEXT   See *Perspective-taking sense of self.*

THE PRESENT MOMENT   Flexible attention to and ongoing nonjudgmental contact with psychological and environmental events as they occur.

TRANSCENDENT SENSE OF SELF   See *Perspective-taking sense of self.*

TRANSFORMATION OF STIMULUS FUNCTIONS   A defining feature of relational frames that refers to the modification of the stimulus functions of related events based on contextual cues that specify a relevant function and the relational frame that these events participate in.

VALUES   Freely chosen, verbally constructed consequences of ongoing, dynamic, evolving patterns of activity, that establish predominant reinforcers for that activity that are present, intrinsic qualities of the valued behavioral pattern itself.

VERBAL EVENTS   Events that have their functions because they participate in relational frames. In this use, *verbal* can be used to qualify any other term (e.g., stimuli, behavior, reinforcers, antecedents, understanding) to refer to that source of functions.

Suggested Readings
and Other Materials

Those wishing to learn how to do acceptance and commitment therapy (ACT) should do six things.

1. Take advantage of the vast amount of materials at the Association for Contextual Behavioral Science (ACBS) website (http://www.contextual psychology.org).

2. Read the second edition of the original ACT book, which describes the theory and method in detail:

   Hayes, S. C., Strosahl, K., & Wilson, K. G. (2011). *Acceptance and commitment therapy: The practice and process of mindful change* (2nd ed.) New York, NY: Guilford Press.

   Then read the following volume:

   Luoma, J., Hayes, S. C., & Walser, R. (2007). *Learning ACT.* Oakland, CA: New Harbinger. [This is a step-by-step guide to ACT methods. It is very practical and helpful.]

3. Read a general ACT self-help book and apply the methods to yourself. The two most popular are:

    Hayes, S. C., & Smith, S. (2005). *Get out of your mind and into your life.* Oakland, CA: New Harbinger.
    Harris, R. (2008). *The happiness trap.* New York, NY: Shambhala.

4. Watch ACT DVDs. The present volume is designed to work in combination with this therapy-skills DVD, produced with a real client:

    Hayes, S. C. (2009). *Acceptance and commitment therapy* (DVD). Washington, DC: American Psychological Association.

    Another good set of DVD materials is:

    Hayes, S. C. (Ed.). (2007). *ACT in action* (DVD series). Oakland, CA: New Harbinger. [This set of six DVDs focuses on specific psychological flexibility processes and key issues. The six topic titles are: Facing the Struggle; Control and Acceptance; Cognitive Defusion; Mindfulness, Self, and Contact with the Present Moment; Values and Action; and Psychological Flexibility. Focusing on a specific process is a bit artificial (a normal ACT session would move from process to process based on clinical need), but it does help in learning. The sessions involve several ACT therapists from around the world in addition to Steve Hayes, including Ann Bailey-Ciarrochi, JoAnne Dahl, Rainer Sonntag, Kirk Strosahl, Robyn Walser, Rikard Wicksell, and Kelly Wilson, showing their respective styles.]

5. Attend at least two different ACT workshops, at least one of which is personally focused and experiential. The ACBS maintains a list of worldwide trainings on its website. Experiential and personal work is critical to using ACT appropriately, and we suggest at least two workshops in order to see the variety of styles that can be applied to this work.

6. Finally, apply the methods with clients, drawing on specific books that fit the kinds of clients you work with. After a few manualized cases, you can put the manual aside and try to work on a more session-to-session and moment-to-moment basis as a functional approach, but following a thorough manual first will push you into corners of the work you may not yet know how to master. Here are several key volumes of the many available. The ACBS website offers a comprehensive list.

Dahl, J., Wilson, K. G., Luciano, C., & Hayes, S. C. (2005). *Acceptance and commitment therapy for chronic pain.* Oakland, CA: New Harbinger/Context Press. [Describes an ACT approach to chronic pain. Very accessible and readable. One of the better clinical expositions on how to do ACT values work.]

Eifert, G., & Forsyth, J. (2005). *Acceptance and commitment therapy for anxiety disorders.* Oakland, CA: New Harbinger. [Good book with a protocol that shows how to mix a variety of ACT processes into a brief therapy for anxiety disorders.]

Hayes, S. C., & Strosahl, K. D. (2005). *A practical guide to acceptance and commitment therapy.* New York, NY: Springer-Verlag. [Shows how to do ACT with a variety of populations.]

McCracken, L. M. (2005). *Contextual cognitive-behavioral therapy for chronic pain.* Seattle, WA: International Association for the Study of Pain. [Describes an interdisciplinary ACT-based approach to chronic pain.]

Walser, R., & Westrup, D. (2007). *Acceptance & commitment therapy for the treatment of post-traumatic stress disorder & trauma-related problems: A practitioner's guide to using mindfulness & acceptance strategies.* Oakland, CA: New Harbinger. [A very practical and accessible approach to using ACT to treat posttraumatic stress disorder and acute trauma-related symptoms.]

Wilson, K. G., & Dufrene, T. (2009). *Mindfulness for two: An acceptance and commitment therapy approach to mindfulness in psychotherapy.* Oakland, CA: New Harbinger. [A book on ACT that emphasizes mindfulness and the therapeutic relationship.]

Zettle, R. (2007). *ACT for depression: A clinician's guide to using acceptance & commitment therapy in treating depression.* Oakland, CA: New Harbinger. [A solid book from one of the founders of ACT.]

References

American Psychological Association, Division 12, Society of Clinical Psychology, (n.d.). [Studies in the areas of depression and chronic pain]. Retrieved from http://www.div12.org/PsychologicalTreatments/treatments.html

Association for Contextual Behavioral Science (ACBS), (n.d.). [List of core competencies]. Retrieved from http://contextualpsychology.org/act_session_checklist; [List of empirical publications in ACT, RFT, and psychological flexibility]. Retrieved from http://contextualpsychology.org/state_of_the_act_evidence; [List of experimental studies linked to the RFT research program in basic behavioral psychology]. Retrieved from www.contextualpsychology.org/rft_empirical_support

Bach, P., & Hayes, S. C. (2002). The use of Acceptance and Commitment Therapy to prevent the rehospitalization of psychotic patients: A randomized controlled trial. *Journal of Consulting and Clinical Psychology, 70,* 1129–1139. doi:10.1037/0022-006X.70.5.1129

Baer, R. A. (2003). Mindfulness training as a clinical intervention: A conceptual and empirical review. *Clinical Psychology: Science and Practice, 10,* 125–143. doi:10.1093/clipsy.bpg015

Baer, R. A. (Ed.). (2006). *Mindfulness-based treatment approaches: Clinician's guide to evidence base and applications.* San Diego, CA: Elsevier.

Barnes-Holmes, D., Hayden, E., Barnes-Holmes, Y., & Stewart, I. (2008). The Implicit Relational Assessment Procedure (IRAP) as a response-time and event-related-potentials methodology for testing natural verbal relations: A preliminary study. *The Psychological Record, 58,* 497–516.

Barnes-Holmes, D., Murphy, A., Barnes-Holmes, Y., & Stewart, I. (2010). The Implicit Relational Assessment Procedure (IRAP): Exploring the impact of private versus public contexts and the response latency criterion on pro-white and anti-black stereotyping among white Irish individuals. *The Psychological Record, 60,* 57–80.

Barnes-Holmes, D., Murtagh, L., Barnes-Holmes, Y., & Stewart, I. (2010). Using the Implicit Association Test and the Implicit Relational Assessment Procedure to measure attitudes towards meat and vegetables in vegetarians and meat-eaters. *The Psychological Record, 60,* 287–306.

Barnes-Holmes, D., Regan, D., Barnes-Holmes, Y., Commins, S., Walsh, D., Stewart, I., . . . Dymond, S. (2005). Relating derived relations as a model of analogical reasoning: Reaction times and event-related potentials. *Journal of the Experimental Analysis of Behavior, 84,* 435–451. doi:10.1901/jeab.2005.79-04

Barnes-Holmes, D., Staunton, C., Barnes-Holmes, Y., Whelan, R., Stewart, I., Commins, S., . . . Dymond, S. (2004). Interfacing Relational Frame Theory with cognitive neuroscience: Semantic priming, The Implicit Association Test, and event related potentials. *International Journal of Psychology & Psychological Therapy, 4,* 215–240.

Berens, N. M., & Hayes, S. C. (2007). Arbitrarily applicable comparative relations: Experimental evidence for a relational operant. *Journal of Applied Behavior Analysis, 40,* 45–71. doi:10.1901/jaba.2007.7-06

Biglan, A., & Hayes, S. C. (1996). Should the behavioral sciences become more pragmatic? The case for functional contextualism in research on human behavior. *Applied & Preventive Psychology, 5,* 47–57.

Brown, L. A., Forman, E. M., Herbert, J. D., Hoffman, K. L., Yuen, E. K., & Goetter, E. M. (2011). A randomized controlled trial of acceptance-based behavior therapy and cognitive therapy for test anxiety: A pilot study. *Behavior Modification, 35,* 31–53. doi:10.1177/0145445510390930

Cassidy, S., Roche, B., & Hayes, S. C. (2011). A relational frame training intervention to raise intelligence quotients: A pilot study. *The Psychological Record, 61,* 173–198.

Chambers, R., Chuen Yee Lo, B., & Allen, N. B. (2008). The impact of intensive mindfulness training on attentional control, cognitive style, and affect. *Cognitive Therapy and Research, 32,* 303–322. doi:10.1007/s10608-007-9119-0

Chawla, N., & Ostafin, B. D. (2007). Experiential avoidance as a functional dimensional approach to psychopathology: An empirical review. *Journal of Clinical Psychology, 63,* 871–890. doi:10.1002/jclp.20400

Christensen, A., Jacobson, N. S., & Babcock, J. C. (1995). Integrative behavioral couple therapy. In N. S. Jacobson & A. S. Gurman (Eds.), *Clinical handbook of couples therapy* (pp. 31–64). New York, NY: Guilford Press.

Cochrane, A., Barnes-Holmes, D., Barnes-Holmes, Y., Stewart, I., & Luciano, C. (2007). Experiential avoidance and aversive visual images: Response delays and event related potentials on a simple matching task. *Behaviour Research and Therapy, 45,* 1379–1388. doi:10.1016/j.brat.2006.05.010

Cook, D., & Hayes, S. C. (2010). Acceptance-based coping and the psychological adjustment of Asian and Caucasian Americans. *International Journal of Behavioral Consultation and Therapy, 6,* 186–197.

David, D., & Montgomery, G. H. (2011). The scientific status of psychotherapies: A new evaluative framework for evidenced-based psychosocial interventions. *Clinical Psychology: Science and Practice, 18,* 89–99. doi:10.1111/j.1468-2850.2011.01239.x

Davis, R. N., & Nolen-Hoeksema, S. (2000). Cognitive inflexibility among ruminators and nonruminators. *Cognitive Therapy and Research, 24,* 699–711. doi:10.1023/A:1005591412406

De Houwer, J. (2011). Why the cognitive approach in psychology would profit from a functional approach and vice versa. *Perspectives on Psychological Science, 6,* 202–209. doi:10.1177/1745691611400238

Dimidjian, S., Hollon, S. D., Dobson, K. S., Schmaling, K. B., Kohlenberg, R. J., . . . Jacobson, N. S. (2006). Randomized trial of behavioral activation, cognitive therapy, and antidepressant medication in the acute treatment of adults with major depression. *Journal of Consulting and Clinical Psychology, 74,* 658–670. doi:10.1037/0022-006X.74.4.658

Dimidjian, S., Kleiber, B. V., & Segal, Z. V. (2009). Mindfulness-based cognitive therapy. In N. Kazantsis, M. A. Reinecke, & A. Freeman (Eds.), *Cognitive and behavioral theories in clinical practice* (pp. 307–330). New York, NY: Guilford.

Fletcher, L., & Hayes, S. C. (2005). Relational Frame Theory, Acceptance and Commitment Therapy, and a functional analytic definition of mindfulness. *Journal of Rational-Emotive & Cognitive Behavior Therapy, 23,* 315–336. doi:10.1007/s10942-005-0017-7

Fletcher, L. B., Schoendorff, B., & Hayes, S. C. (2010). Searching for mindfulness in the brain: A process-oriented approach to examining the neural correlates of mindfulness. *Mindfulness, 1,* 41–63. doi:10.1007/s12671-010-0006-5

Franks, C. M., & Wilson, G. T. (1974). *Annual review of behavior therapy: Theory and practice* (Vol. 1). New York, NY: Brunner/Mazel.

Freud, S. (1928/1955). Analyse d'une phobie chez un petit garçon de cinq ans (Le petit Hans.) [Analysis of a phobia in a five-year-old boy (little Hans)], *Revue Française de Psychanalyse, 2*(3). Reprinted in *The complete psychological works of Sigmund Freud,* Vol. 10, James Strachey, Trans. London, England: Hogarth.

Gaudiano, B. A. (2009). Öst's (2008) methodological comparison of clinical trials of Acceptance and Commitment Therapy versus Cognitive Behavior Therapy: Matching apples with oranges? *Behaviour Research and Therapy, 47,* 1066–1070. doi:10.1016/j.brat.2009.07.020

Gaudiano, B. A., & Herbert, J. D. (2006). Acute treatment of inpatients with psychotic symptoms using Acceptance and Commitment Therapy. *Behaviour Research and Therapy, 44,* 415–437. doi:10.1016/j.brat.2005.02.007

Gifford, E. V., Kohlenberg, B., Hayes, S. C., Pierson, H., Piasecki, M., Antonuccio, D., & Palm, K. (2011). Does acceptance and relationship focused behavior therapy contribute to bupropion outcomes? A randomized controlled trial of FAP and ACT for smoking cessation. *Behavior Therapy, 42,* 700–715. doi:10.1016/j.beth.2011.03.002

Gregg, J. A., Callaghan, G. M., Hayes, S. C., & Glenn-Lawson, J. L. (2007). Improving diabetes self-management through acceptance, mindfulness, and values: A randomized controlled trial. *Journal of Consulting and Clinical Psychology, 75,* 336–343. doi:10.1037/0022-006X.75.2.336

Griner, D., & Smith, T. B. (2006). Culturally adapted mental health intervention: A meta-analytic review. *Psychotherapy: Theory, Research, Practice, Training, 43,* 531–548. doi:10.1037/0033-3204.43.4.531

Haeffel, G. J. (2010). When self-help is no help: Traditional cognitive skills training does not prevent depressive symptoms in people who ruminate. *Behaviour Research and Therapy, 48,* 152–157. doi:10.1016/j.brat.2009.09.016

Hall, G. C. N., Hong, J. J., Zane, N. W. S., & Meyer, O. L. (2011). Culturally-competent treatments for Asian Americans: The relevance of mindfulness and acceptance-based psychotherapies. *Clinical Psychology: Science and Practice, 18,* 215–231. doi:10.1111/j.1468-2850.2011.01253.x

Hayes, S. C. (1982, October). *Cognitive distancing and psychopathology.* Presentation to Broughton Hospital, Morganton, NC.

Hayes, S. C. (Ed.). (1989). *Rule-governed behavior: Cognition, contingencies, and instructional control.* New York, NY: Plenum.

Hayes, S. C. (2004a). Acceptance and Commitment Therapy, Relational Frame Theory, and the third wave of behavior therapy. *Behavior Therapy, 35,* 639–665. doi:10.1016/S0005-7894(04)80013-3

Hayes, S. C. (2004b). Acceptance and Commitment Therapy and the new behavior therapies: Mindfulness, acceptance and relationship. In S. C. Hayes, V. M. Follette, & M. Linehan (Eds.), *Mindfulness and acceptance: Expanding the cognitive behavioral tradition* (pp. 1–29). New York, NY: Guilford.

Hayes, S. C. (Ed.). (2007). *ACT in action.* Oakland, CA: New Harbinger.

Hayes, S. C. (2009). *Acceptance and commitment therapy* (DVD). Washington, DC: American Psychological Association.

Hayes, S. C., Barnes-Holmes, D., & Roche, B. (2001). *Relational Frame Theory: A Post-Skinnerian account of human language and cognition.* New York, NY: Plenum Press.

Hayes, S. C., Bissett, R., Korn, Z., Zettle, R. D., Rosenfarb, I., Cooper, L., & Grundt, A. (1999). The impact of acceptance versus control rationales on pain tolerance. *The Psychological Record, 49,* 33–47.

Hayes, S. C., Bissett, R., Roget, N., Padilla, M., Kohlenberg, B. S., Fisher, G., . . . Niccolls, R. (2004). The impact of acceptance and commitment training and multicultural training on the stigmatizing attitudes and professional burnout of substance abuse counselors. *Behavior Therapy, 35,* 821–835. doi:10.1016/S0005-7894(04)80022-4

Hayes, S. C., Brownstein, A. J., Haas, J. R., & Greenway, D. E. (1986). Instructions, multiple schedules, and extinction: Distinguishing rule-governed from schedule controlled behavior. *Journal of the Experimental Analysis of Behavior, 46,* 137–147. doi:10.1901/jeab.1986.46-137

Hayes, S. C., Brownstein, A. J., Zettle, R. D., Rosenfarb, I., & Korn, Z. (1986). Rule-governed behavior and sensitivity to changing consequences of responding. *Journal of the Experimental Analysis of Behavior, 45,* 237–256. doi:10.1901/jeab.1986.45-237

Hayes, S. C., Hayes, L. J., & Reese, H. W. (1988). Finding the philosophical core: A review of Stephen C. Pepper's *World Hypotheses. Journal of the Experimental Analysis of Behavior, 50,* 97–111. doi:10.1901/jeab.1988.50-97

Hayes, S. C., Hayes, L. J., Reese, H. W., & Sarbin, T. R. (Eds.). (1993). *Varieties of scientific contextualism.* Reno, NV: Context Press.

Hayes, S. C., Levin, M., Plumb, J., Boulanger, J., & Pistorello, J. (in press). Acceptance and Commitment Therapy and contextual behavioral science: Examining the progress of a distinctive model of behavioral and cognitive therapy. *Behavior Therapy.* Retrieved from http://www.journals.elsevier.com/behavior-therapy/

Hayes, S. C., Levin, M., Vilardaga, R., & Yadavaia, J. (2008, September). *A meta-analysis of mediational and component analyses of ACT.* Paper presented to the European Association for Behavioral and Cognitive Therapies Annual Congress, Helsinki, Finland.

Hayes, S. C., Luoma, J., Bond, F., Masuda, A., & Lillis, J. (2006). Acceptance and Commitment Therapy: Model, processes, and outcomes. *Behaviour Research and Therapy, 44,* 1–25. doi:10.1016/j.brat.2005.06.006

Hayes, S. C., & Nelson, R. O. (1983). Similar reactivity produced by external cues and self-monitoring. *Behavior Modification, 7,* 183–196. doi:10.1177/01454455830072004

Hayes, S. C., Muto, T., & Masuda, A. (2011). Seeking cultural competence from the ground up. *Clinical Psychology: Science and Practice, 18,* 232–237. doi:10.1111/j.1468-2850.2011.01254.x

Hayes, S. C., Rincover, A., & Volosin, D. (1980). Variables influencing the acquisition and maintenance of aggressive behavior: Modeling versus sensory reinforcement. *Journal of Abnormal Psychology, 89,* 254–262. doi:10.1037/0021-843X.89.2.254

Hayes, S. C., Rosenfarb, I., Wulfert, E., Munt, E., Zettle, R. D., & Korn, Z. (1985). Self-reinforcement effects: An artifact of social standard setting? *Journal of Applied Behavior Analysis, 18,* 201–214. doi:10.1901/jaba.1985.18-201

Hayes, S. C., & Smith, S. (2005). *Get out of your mind and into your life: The new Acceptance and Commitment Therapy.* Oakland, CA: New Harbinger.

Hayes, S. C., Strosahl, K., & Wilson, K. G. (1999). *Acceptance and Commitment Therapy: An experiential approach to behavior change.* New York, NY: Guilford Press.

Hayes, S. C., Strosahl, K., & Wilson, K. G. (2011). *Acceptance and Commitment Therapy: The process and practice of mindful change* (2nd ed.). New York, NY: Guilford Press.

Hayes, S. C., Villatte, M., Levin, M., & Hildebrandt, M. (2011). Open, aware, and active: Contextual approaches as an emerging trend in the behavioral and cognitive therapies. *Annual Review of Clinical Psychology, 7,* 141–168. doi:10.1146/annurev-clinpsy-032210-104449

Hayes, S. C., Wilson, K. G., Gifford, E. V., Bissett, R., Piasecki, M., Batten, S. V., . . . Gregg, J. (2004). A randomized controlled trial of twelve-step facilitation and acceptance and commitment therapy with polysubstance abusing methadone maintained opiate addicts. *Behavior Therapy, 35,* 667–688. doi:10.1016/S0005-7894(04)80014-5

Hayes, S. C., Wilson, K. W., Gifford, E. V., Follette, V. M., & Strosahl, K. (1996). Experiential avoidance and behavioral disorders: A functional dimensional approach to diagnosis and treatment. *Journal of Consulting and Clinical Psychology, 64,* 1152–1168. doi:10.1037/0022-006X.64.6.1152

Hayes, S. C., & Wolf, M. R. (1984). Cues, consequences, and therapeutic talk: Effect of social context and coping statements on pain. *Behaviour Research and Therapy, 22,* 385–392. doi:10.1016/0005-7967(84)90081-0

Hayes, S. C., Zettle, R. D., & Rosenfarb, I. (1989). Rule following. In S. C. Hayes (Ed.), *Rule-governed behavior: Cognition, contingencies, and instructional control* (pp. 191–220). New York, NY: Plenum.

Holman, E. A., & Silver, R. C. (1998). Getting "stuck" in the past: Temporal orientation and coping with trauma. *Journal of Personality and Social Psychology, 74,* 1146–1163. doi:10.1037/0022-3514.74.5.1146

Hooper, N., Saunders, J., & McHugh, L. (2010). The derived generalization of thought and suppression. *Learning & Behavior, 38,* 160–168. doi:10.3758/LB.38.2.160

Jha, A. P., Krompinger, J., & Baime, M. J. (2007). Mindfulness training modifies subsystems of attention. *Cognitive, Affective, & Behavioral Neuroscience, 7,* 109–119. doi:10.3758/CABN.7.2.109

Ju, W. C., & Hayes, S. C. (2008). Verbal establishing stimuli: Testing the motivative effect of stimuli in a derived relation with consequences. *The Psychological Record, 58,* 339–363.

Kashdan, T. B., Barrios, V., Forsyth, J. P., & Steger, M. F. (2006). Experiential avoidance as a generalized psychological vulnerability: Comparisons with coping and emotion regulation strategies. *Behaviour Research and Therapy, 44,* 1301–1320. doi:10.1016/j.brat.2005.10.003

Kashdan, T. B., & Rottenberg, J. (2010). Psychological flexibility as a fundamental aspect of health. *Clinical Psychology Review, 30,* 865–878. doi:10.1016/j.cpr.2010.03.001

Kishita, N., & Shimada, H. (2011). Effects of acceptance-based coping on task performance and subjective stress. *Journal of Behavior Therapy and Experimental Psychiatry, 42,* 6–12. doi:10.1016/j.jbtep.2010.08.005

Kohlenberg, R. J., & Tsai, M. (1991). *Functional analytic psychotherapy.* New York, NY: Plenum Press.

Lappalainen, R., Lehtonen, T., Skarp, E., Taubert, E., Ojanen, M., & Hayes, S. C. (2007). The impact of CBT and ACT models using psychology trainee therapists: A preliminary controlled effectiveness trial. *Behavior Modification, 31,* 488–511. doi:10.1177/0145445506298436

Levin, M., & Hayes, S. C. (2009). Is Acceptance and Commitment Therapy superior to established treatment comparisons? *Psychotherapy and Psychosomatics, 78,* 380. doi:10.1159/000235978

Levin, M., Hayes, S. C., & Waltz, T. (2010). Creating an implicit measure of cognition more suited to applied research: A test of the Mixed Trial—Implicit Relational Assessment Procedure (MT-IRAP). *International Journal of Behavioral Consultation and Therapy, 6,* 245–262.

Levin, M., Hildebrandt, M., Lillis, J., & Hayes, S. C. (2012). *The impact of treatment components in Acceptance and Commitment Therapy: A meta-analysis of micro-component studies.* Manuscript submitted for publication.

Lillis, J., & Hayes, S. C. (2007). Applying acceptance, mindfulness, and values to the reduction of prejudice: A pilot study. *Behavior Modification, 31,* 389–411. doi:10.1177/0145445506298413

Lillis, J., Hayes, S. C., Bunting, K., & Masuda, A. (2009). Teaching acceptance and mindfulness to improve the lives of the obese: A preliminary test of a theoretical model. *Annals of Behavioral Medicine, 37,* 58–69. doi:10.1007/s12160-009-9083-x

Linehan, M. M. (1993). *Cognitive-behavioral treatment of borderline personality disorder.* New York, NY: Guilford Press.

Lipkens, R., & Hayes, S. C. (2009). Producing and recognizing analogical relations. *Journal of the Experimental Analysis of Behavior, 91,* 105–126. doi:10.1901/jeab.2009.91-105

Lipkens, R., Hayes, S. C., & Hayes, L. J. (1993). Longitudinal study of derived stimulus relations in an infant. *Journal of Experimental Child Psychology, 56,* 201–239. doi:10.1006/jecp.1993.1032

Longmore, R. J., & Worrell, M. (2007). Do we need to challenge thoughts in cognitive behavioral therapy? *Clinical Psychology Review, 27,* 173–187. doi:10.1016/j.cpr.2006.08.001

Luciano, C., Gómez-Becerra, I., & Rodríguez-Valverde, M. (2007). The role of multiple-exemplar training and naming in establishing derived equivalence in an infant. *Journal of the Experimental Analysis of Behavior, 87,* 349–365. doi:10.1901/jeab.2007.08-06

Lundgren, T., Dahl, J., Melin, L., & Kees, B. (2006). Evaluation of Acceptance and Commitment Therapy for drug refractory epilepsy: A randomized controlled trial in South Africa. *Epilepsia, 47,* 2173–2179. doi:10.1111/j.1528-1167.2006.00892.x

Lundgren, T., Dahl, J., Yardi, N., & Melin, L. (2008). Acceptance and Commitment Therapy and yoga for drug-refractory epilepsy: A randomized controlled trial. *Epilepsy & Behavior, 13,* 102–108. doi:10.1016/j.yebeh.2008.02.009

Luoma, J., Hayes, S. C., & Walser, R. (2007). *Learning ACT.* Oakland, CA: New Harbinger.

Luoma, J., Kohlenberg, B., Hayes, S. C., & Fletcher, L. (2012). Slow and steady wins the race: A randomized clinical trial of Acceptance and Commitment Therapy targeting shame in substance use disorders. *Journal of Consulting and Clinical Psychology, 80,* 43–53. doi:10.1037/a0026070

Martell, C. R., Dimidjian, S., & Herman-Dunn, R. (2010). *Behavioral activation for depression: A clinician's guide.* New York, NY: Guilford.

Masuda, A., Hayes, S. C., Fletcher, L. B., Seignourel, P. J., Bunting, K., Herbst, S. A., . . . Lillis, J. (2007). The impact of Acceptance and Commitment Therapy versus education on stigma toward people with psychological disorders. *Behaviour Research and Therapy, 45,* 2764–2772. doi:10.1016/j.brat.2007.05.008

Masuda, A., Hayes, S. C., Twohig, M. P., Drossel, C., Lillis, J., & Washio, Y. (2008). A parametric study of cognitive defusion and the believability and discomfort of negative self-relevant thoughts. *Behavior Modification, 33,* 250–262. doi:10.1177/0145445508326259

Masuda, A., Muto, T., Hayes, S. C., & Lillis, J. (2008). Acceptance and commitment therapy: Application to a Japanese client. *Japanese Journal of Behavior Therapy, 34,* 137–148.

Masuda, A., Wendell, J. W., Chou, Y., & Feinstein, A. B. (2010). Relationships among self-concealment, mindfulness, and negative psychological outcomes in

Asian American and European American college students. *International Journal for the Advancement of Counselling, 32,* 165–177. doi:10.1007/s10447-010-9097-x

McHugh, L., Barnes-Holmes, Y., & Barnes-Holmes, D. (2004). Perspective-taking as relational responding: A developmental profile. *The Psychological Record, 54,* 115–144.

McHugh, L., Barnes-Holmes, Y., Barnes-Holmes, D., & Stewart, I. (2006). Understanding false belief as generalized operant behaviour. *The Psychological Record, 56,* 341–364.

McHugh, L., Barnes-Holmes, Y., Barnes-Holmes, D., Stewart, I., & Dymond, S. (2007). Deictic relational complexity and the development of deception. *The Psychological Record, 57,* 517–531.

McHugh, L., Barnes-Holmes, Y., Barnes-Holmes, D., Whelan, R., & Stewart, I. (2007). Knowing me, knowing you: Deictic complexity in false-belief understanding. *The Psychological Record, 57,* 533–542.

McMullen, J., Barnes-Holmes, D., Barnes-Holmes, Y., Stewart, I., Luciano, C., & Cochrane, A. (2008). Acceptance versus distraction: Brief instructions, metaphors, and exercises in increasing tolerance for self-delivered electric shocks. *Behaviour Research and Therapy, 46,* 122–129. doi:10.1016/j.brat.2007.09.002

Muto, T., Hayes, S. C., & Jeffcoat, T. (2011). The effectiveness of Acceptance and Commitment Therapy bibliotherapy for enhancing the psychological health of Japanese college students living abroad. *Behavior Therapy, 42,* 323–335. doi:10.1016/j.beth.2010.08.009

Nagayama Hall, G. C., Hong, J. J., Zane, N. W., & Meyer, O. L. (2011). Culturally-competent treatments for Asian Americans: The relevance of mindfulness and acceptance-based psychotherapies. *Clinical Psychology, 18,* 215–231.

Nelson, R. O., & Hayes, S. C. (1981). Theoretical explanations for the reactive effects of self-monitoring. *Behavior Modification, 5,* 3–14. doi:10.1177/014544558151001

Nelson, R. O., Hayes, S. C., Spong, R. T., Jarrett, R. B., & McKnight, D. L. (1983). Self-reinforcement: Appealing misnomer or effective mechanism? *Behaviour Research and Therapy, 21,* 557–566. doi:10.1016/0005-7967(83)90047-5

Nowak, M. A., Tarnita, C. E., & Wilson, E. O. (2010, August 26). The evolution of eusociality. *Nature, 466,* 1057–1062. doi:10.1038/nature09205

Öst, L.-G. (2008). Efficacy of the third wave of behavioral therapies: A systematic review and meta-analysis. *Behaviour Research and Therapy, 46,* 296–321. doi:10.1016/j.brat.2007.12.005

O'Toole, C., & Barnes-Holmes, D. (2009). Three chronometric indices of relational responding as predictors of performance on a brief intelligence test: The importance of relational flexibility. *The Psychological Record, 59,* 119–132.

Pankey, J. (2008). *Acceptance and Commitment Therapy with dually diagnosed individuals.* Unpublished doctoral dissertation, University of Nevada, Reno.

Pepper, S. C. (1942). *World hypotheses: A study in evidence.* Berkeley: University of California Press.

Pierson, H., & Hayes, S. C. (2007). Using Acceptance and Commitment Therapy to empower the therapeutic relationship. In P. Gilbert & R. Leahy (Eds.), *The therapeutic relationship in cognitive behavior therapy* (pp. 205–228). London, England: Routledge.

Plumb, J. C., & Vilardaga, R. (2010). Assessing treatment integrity in Acceptance and Commitment Therapy: Strategies and suggestions. *International Journal of Behavioral Consultation and Therapy, 6,* 263–295.

Polusny, M. A., Ries, B. J., Meis, L. A., DeGarmo, D., McCormick-Deaton, C. M., Thuras, P., & Erbes, C. R. (2011). Effects of parents' experiential avoidance and PTSD on adolescent disaster-related posttraumatic stress symptomatology. *Journal of Family Psychology, 25,* 220–229. doi:10.1037/a0022945

Powers, M. B., Vörding, M., & Emmelkamp, P. M. G. (2009). Acceptance and commitment therapy: A meta-analytic review. *Psychotherapy and Psychosomatics, 78,* 73–80. doi:10.1159/000190790

Pull, C. B. (2009). Current empirical status of acceptance and commitment therapy. *Current Opinion in Psychiatry, 22*(1), 55–60. doi:10.1097YCO.0b013e32831a6e9d

Rosales, R., & Rehfeldt, R. A. (2007). Contriving transitive conditioned establishing operations to establish derived manding skills in adults with severe developmental disabilities. *Journal of Applied Behavior Analysis, 40,* 105–121. doi:10.1901/jaba.2007.117-05

Rosenfarb, I., & Hayes, S. C. (1984). Social standard setting: The Achilles' heel of informational accounts of therapeutic change. *Behavior Therapy, 15,* 515–528. doi:10.1016/S0005-7894(84)80053-2

Rosenfarb, I. S., Hayes, S. C., & Linehan, M. M. (1989). Instructions and experiential feedback in the treatment of social skills deficits in adults. *Psychotherapy: Theory, Research, Practice, Training, 26,* 242–251. doi:10.1037/h0085425

Ruiz, F. J. (2010). A review of Acceptance and Commitment Therapy (ACT) empirical evidence: Correlational, experimental psychopathology, component and outcome studies. *International Journal of Psychology & Psychological Therapy, 10,* 125–162.

Segal, Z. V., Teasdale, J. D., & Williams, J. M. G. (2004). Mindfulness-based cognitive therapy: Theoretical rationale and empirical status. In S. C. Hayes, V. M. Follette, & M. M. Linehan (Eds.), *Mindfulness and acceptance: Expanding the cognitive-behavioral tradition* (pp. 45–65). New York, NY: Guilford Press.

Segal, Z. V., Williams, J. M. G., & Teasdale, J. D. (2002). *Mindfulness-based cognitive therapy for depression: A new approach to preventing relapse.* New York, NY: Guilford Press.

Sheldon, K. M., Ryan, R., Deci, E., & Kasser, T. (2004). The independent effects of goal contents and motives on well-being: It's both what you pursue and why you pursue it. *Personality and Social Psychology Bulletin, 30,* 475–486. doi:10.1177/0146167203261883

Stewart, I., Barnes-Holmes, D., & Roche, B. (2004). A functional-analytic model of analogy using the relational evaluation procedure. *The Psychological Record, 54,* 531–552.

Strosahl, K. D., Hayes, S. C., Wilson, K. G., & Gifford, E. V. (2004). An ACT primer: Core therapy processes, intervention strategies, and therapist competencies. In S. C. Hayes & K. D. Strosahl (Eds.), *A practical guide to Acceptance and Commitment Therapy* (pp. 31–58). New York, NY: Springer-Verlag.

Sue, S., Zane, N., Nagayama Hall, G. C., & Berger, L. K. (2009). The case for cultural competency in psychotherapeutic interventions. *Annual Review of Psychology, 60,* 525–548. doi:10.1146/annurev.psych.60.110707.163651

Sylvester, M. (2011). *Examining the feasibility and efficacy of modified acceptance and commitment therapy for improving adaptive functioning in persons with a history of pediatric acquired brain injury.* Unpublished doctoral dissertation, University of Nevada, Reno.

Takahashi, M., Muto, T., Tada, M., & Sugiyama, M. (2002). Acceptance rationale and increasing pain tolerance: Acceptance-based and FEAR-based practice. *Japanese Journal of Behavior Therapy, 28,* 35–46.

U.S. Substance Abuse and Mental Health Services Administration, National Registry of Evidence-Based Programs and Practices. (n.d.). [Studies cited in areas of psychosis, worksite stress, and obsessive–compulsive disorder]. Retrieved from http://174.140.153.167/ViewIntervention.aspx?id=191

Vilardaga, R., Estévez, A., Levin, M. E., & Hayes, S. C. (in press). Deictic relational responding, empathy and experiential avoidance as predictors of social anhedonia: Further contributions from relational frame theory. *The Psychological Record.*

Vilardaga, R., Hayes, S. C., Levin, M. E., & Muto, T. (2009). Creating a strategy for progress: A contextual behavioral science approach. *The Behavior Analyst, 32,* 105–133.

Wampold, B. E. (2001). *The great psychotherapy debate: Models, methods, and findings.* Mahwah, NJ: Erlbaum.

Weil, T. M., Hayes, S. C., & Capurro, P. (2011). Establishing a deictic relational repertoire in young children. *The Psychological Record, 61,* 371–390.

Wells, A. (2000). *Emotional disorders & metacognition: Innovative cognitive therapy.* Chichester, England: Wiley.

Wells, A. (2008). Metacognitive therapy: Cognition applied to regulating cognition. *Behavioural and Cognitive Psychotherapy, 36,* 651–658. doi:10.1017/S1352465808004803

Wenzlaff, R. M., & Wegner, D. M. (2000). Thought suppression. *Annual Review of Psychology, 51,* 59–91. doi:10.1146/annurev.psych.51.1.59

Westin, V. Z., Schulin, M., Hesser, H., Karlsson, M., Noe, R. Z., Olofsson, U., . . . Andersson, G. (2011). Acceptance and Commitment Therapy versus Tinnitus Retraining Therapy in the treatment of tinnitus distress: A randomized controlled trial. *Behaviour Research and Therapy, 49,* 737–747. doi:10.1016/j.brat.2011.08.001

Wetherell, J. L., Liua, L., Patterson, T. L., Afari, N., Ayers, C. R., Thorp, S. R., . . . Petkus, A. J. (2011). Acceptance and Commitment Therapy for generalized anxiety disorder in older adults: A preliminary report. *Behavior Therapy, 42,* 127–134. doi:10.1016/j.beth.2010.07.002

Wicksell, R. K., Melin, L., Lekander, M., & Olsson, G. L. (2009). Evaluating the effectiveness of exposure and acceptance strategies to improve functioning and quality of life in longstanding pediatric pain—A randomized controlled trial. *Pain, 141,* 248–257. doi:10.1016/j.pain.2008.11.006

Wicksell, R. K., Melin, L., & Olsson, G. L. (2007). Exposure and acceptance in the rehabilitation of adolescents with idiopathic chronic pain: A pilot study. *European Journal of Pain, 11*(3), 267–274. doi:10.1016/j.ejpain.2006.02.012

Wolpe, J., & Rachman, S. (1960). Psychoanalytic "evidence": A critique based on Freud's case of little Hans. *Journal of Nervous and Mental Disease, 131,* 135–148. doi:10.1097/00005053-196008000-00007

Yadavaia, J. E., & Hayes, S. C. (in press). Acceptance and Commitment Therapy for self-stigma around sexual orientation: A multiple baseline evaluation. *Cognitive and Behavioral Practice.*

Zettle, R. D. (2003). Acceptance and commitment therapy (ACT) versus systematic desensitization in treatment of mathematics anxiety. *The Psychological Record, 53,* 197–215.

Zettle, R. D., & Hayes, S. C. (1983). Effect of social context on the impact of coping self-statements. *Psychological Reports, 52,* 391–401. doi:10.2466/pr0.1983.52.2.391

Zettle, R. D., & Hayes, S. C. (1986). Dysfunctional control by client verbal behavior: The context of reason giving. *The Analysis of Verbal Behavior, 4,* 30–38.

Zettle, R. D., & Rains, J. C. (1989). Group cognitive and contextual therapies in treatment of depression. *Journal of Clinical Psychology, 45,* 436–445. doi:10.1002/1097-4679(198905)45:3<436::AID-JCLP2270450314>3.0.CO;2-L

Zettle, R. D., Rains, J. C., & Hayes, S. C. (2011). Processes of change in Acceptance and Commitment Therapy and Cognitive Therapy for depression: A mediational reanalysis of Zettle and Rains (1989). *Behavior Modification, 35,* 265–283. doi:10.1177/0145445511398344

Index

Ability, cognitive, 125
Absent values, 58–60
ACBS. *See* Association for Contextual
    Behavioral Science
Acceptance
    in acceptance and commitment
        therapy, 6, 7
    of death of loved one, 52–54
    defined, 137
    in defusion techniques, 90–96
    in evidence-based treatments, 39
    experiential avoidance vs., 51–62
    goals of, 92–93
    and openness, 62–63
    of pain, 107–109
    and problem-solving model, 76
    of self and situation, 75–79
Acceptance and commitment therapy
    (ACT). *See also specific headings,*
    e.g.: Evaluation of ACT
    in case example, 8–13
    and cognitive therapy, 122
    defined, 137
    empirical publications in, 117
    as inductive, process-oriented
        approach, 6
    popularity of, 36–37
    and relational frame theory, 123–124

ACT contract, 74
Action, committed. *See* Committed
    action
Active engagement, 62–63, 110–111
Age, 125
Alliance, working, 67
American Psychological Association
    (APA), 37, 45, 118
Anchors, targeted, 114–116
Anxiety
    in case example, 8–13, 75–76
    effectiveness of ACT for, 121
APA. *See* American Psychological
    Association
APA Division 12, 37, 118, 119, 135
Arbitrarily applicable relational
    responding, 137
Arbitrary applicability, 31–32
Assessment, 131–132
Assimilation, 38–39, 130–131
Association, 32
Association for Behavioral and
    Cognitive Therapies, 37
Association for Contextual Behavioral
    Science (ACBS), 36, 38, 117,
    127, 128
Associationism, 18
Attachment, 42, 55–56

About the Authors

Steven C. Hayes, PhD, is Nevada Foundation Professor in the Department of Psychology at the University of Nevada. He is the author of 35 books and over 475 scientific articles. His career has focused on an analysis of the nature of human language and cognition and the application of this to the understanding and alleviation of human suffering. His work has been recognized by several awards, including the Exemplary Contributions to Basic Behavioral Research and Its Applications from the American Psychological Association's Division 25 (Behavior Analysis), the Impact of Science on Application Award from the Society for the Advancement of Behavior Analysis, and the Lifetime Achievement Award from the Association for Behavioral and Cognitive Therapies.

Jason Lillis, PhD, is an instructor in the Department of Psychiatry and Human Behavior at the Warren Alpert Medical School of Brown University and a clinical psychologist at the Weight Control and Diabetes Research Center at The Miriam Hospital. He earned his PhD in clinical psychology from the University of Nevada, Reno, and completed his clinical internship at VA Palo Alto Health Care System, followed by a postdoctoral fellowship in health services research at Stanford University. Dr. Lillis is a leading researcher and an internationally recognized trainer of acceptance and commitment therapy.

About the Series Editors

Jon Carlson, PsyD, EdD, ABPP, is distinguished professor of psychology and counseling at Governors State University in University Park, Illinois, and a psychologist at the Wellness Clinic in Lake Geneva, Wisconsin. Dr. Carlson has served as the editor of several periodicals, including the *Journal of Individual Psychology* and *The Family Journal*. He holds diplomas in both family psychology and Adlerian psychology. He has authored 150 journal articles and 40 books, including *Time for a Better Marriage, Adlerian Therapy, The Mummy at the Dining Room Table, Bad Therapy, The Client Who Changed Me,* and *Moved by the Spirit*. He has created more than 200 professional trade videos and DVDs with leading professional therapists and educators. In 2004 the American Counseling Association named him a "Living Legend." Recently he syndicated an advice cartoon, *On The Edge,* with cartoonist Joe Martin.

Matt Englar-Carlson, PhD, is a professor of counseling at California State University–Fullerton. He is a fellow of Division 51 of the American Psychological Association (APA). As a scholar, teacher, and clinician, Dr. Englar-Carlson has been an innovator and professionally passionate about training and teaching clinicians to work more effectively with their male clients. He has more than 30 publications and 50 national and international presentations, most of which are focused on men and masculinity and diversity issues in psychological training and practice. Dr. Englar-Carlson coedited the books *In the Room With Men: A Casebook of Therapeutic Change* and *Counseling Troubled Boys: A Guidebook for Professionals* and was featured in the 2010 APA-produced DVD *Engaging Men in Psychotherapy*. In 2007, he was named Researcher of the Year by the Society for the Psychological Study of Men and Masculinity. He is also a member of the APA Working Group to Develop Guidelines for Psychological Practice With Boys and Men. As a clinician, he has worked with children, adults, and families in school, community, and university mental health settings.